The
Hymnal
Companion

The Hymnal Companion

Edited By
FRED BOCK
and
BRYAN JEFFERY LEECH

Paragon Associates, Incorporated
Nashville, Tennessee 37202

© Copyright 1979 by Paragon Associates, Inc.
Nashville, TN 37202
International copyright secured. All rights reserved.
ISBN #0-89477-004-7
Printed in the United States of America
10 9 8 7 6 5 4 3 2

Table of Contents

ℱoreword

AN INSIDE LOOK AT THE HYMNAL COMPANION

By Fred Bock

CREATING THE COMPANION to *Hymns for the Family of God* was for me, like the creation of the hymnal itself, an exciting experience. To create this companion we first studied existing companions to other hymnals. Once we saw what others had done, we were better able to evaluate our aims for a *new* hymnal companion. *Hymns for the Family of God* is unlike any other hymnal, so right from the start we had it in the forefront of our minds that our *Companion* should be like no other companion. Most hymnal companions deal with the historicity of hymns and hymntunes, names and dates of authors and composers, and stories surrounding the creation of hymns. Subsequent companions have corrected and codified the information given in previous companions. In this regard, the activities of the Hymn Society of America[1] have been invaluable for they have, since their early beginnings in 1922, encouraged and fostered the research, cataloging and housing of hymn information. Rather than duplicate stories of hymns and hymn creators, we decided to refer you to two excellent reference sources: Donald P. Hustad's *Dictionary-Handbook to "Hymns for the Living Church,"* (Hope Publishing Company, 1978), and William J. Reynolds' *Companion to the Baptist Hymnal*, (Broadman Press, 1976). Others are listed in the "Suggested Books and Periodicals" section of this *Companion*, pages 251-253.

Speaking for my co-editor, Bryan Jeffery Leech, myself, and our Editorial Board, our desire was to create a hymnal companion that would contain information of such value that it would be used often by many folks who want to make the best possible use of their hymnal and its potentials. Let me share with you about this unusual book.

The *Companion* is divided into five parts. Section 1 begins with a Prayer of Dedication: for the hymnal, the hymnal *Companion*, the reader, the minister, the ministers through music, and the congregation—all who

[1]Hymn Society of America, National Headquarters, Wittenburg University, Springfield, OH 45501

come into contact with *Hymns for the Family of God*. This prayer was written by William J. Gaither, a major contributor to the hymnal, and a dear and valued friend. Dr. Howard Stevenson of Westmont College, Santa Barbara, California, has written an article, "A History of Hymns and Their Use." This is interesting reading, not at all stuffy or dull: a good overview of hymnody. Next, in an article dealing with copyright law and the copying music, William Shorney, past President of the Church Music Publishers Association, and Vice-President of Hope Publishing Company, shares new insight into the continuing problem of illegal duplication of copyrighted music in our churches.

Section 2 is entitled *Getting Ready to Worship God,* and deals with constructive and practical ways each of us: minister, minister of music, organist, or congregation member can best prepare to truly worship God. The articles in this section were written by Don G. Fontana, Minister of Music at Garden Grove Community Church, and Director of Music for "Hour of Power" TV production; Dr. Ray E. Robinson, President of Westminster Choir College, Princeton, New Jersey; Fred Bock and Bryan Jeffery Leech, co-editors of this *Companion.* I hope that you will read each one carefully and prayerfully. By rededicating ourselves and our abilities to God Himself, we find we are closer to achieving a strong and vibrant worship experience—individually and corporately.

New Ideas for Exciting Services is the title of the third section. Bryan Jeffery Leech, writer, pastor, composer, speaker, Assistant Editor of *Hymns for the Family of God,* and co-editor of this *Companion,* has put together a wealth of ideas covering every possible subject for the creation of meaningful worship. He has touched upon, and given guidelines for, everything from announcements to decorations to congregational involvement. In this section, Bryan has included special orders of worship for the major holy days: Advent, Christmas, Lent, Palm Sunday, Easter. In addition, he includes services for communion, weddings, memorials, baptism or dedication of children, and many more. There are ten topic-theme ideas for the "every Sunday" kind of services. Of course, much of this service material is based on hymns, Scripture and readings taken from *Hymns for the Family of God.*

The fourth section is entitled *Expanded Use of the Hymnal.* The idea here was to provide a resource bank of available publications that would be helpful to a church musician in making the best possible use of the variety of materials contained in *Hymns for the Family of God.* The first section is by Gloria Gaither, a lyric writer, book writer, wife and mother. Gloria explains and expands a new dimension to *Hymns for the Family of God* none of us predicted. Soon after churches began ordering *Hymns for the Family of God,* we discovered an unusual thing was happening: most would reorder substantial quantities of the hymnal within four to six weeks after their original order had arrived. What we discovered was that members of the congregation wanted them for home use—not just as *hymnbooks*, but as *devotional* books. In her article, Gloria suggests ways in which you and your family can use *Hymns for the Family of God* as a catalyst and resource tool for family devotions. Those of you on the lookout for solo, duet, trio, or quartet selections will be pleased that we asked Douglas Lawrence, noted church musician, recording artist, and a singer who knows how to pick material that works well vocally, to compile this listing. Doug has prepared a comprehensive group of selections contained within *Hymns for the Family of God* that lend themselves especially well to solo, duet, trio or quartet singing. Lucy Hirt, who directed children's choirs for many years at First Presbyterian Church, Hollywood, California, has put together a listing of selections found in the hymnal that she finds can be used as performance material and teaching material as well. Suggested anthems in which children participate along with adult singers are also given. Careful consideration was given to ranges suitable for children's voices, meaningful texts, and combined usefulness as vehicles for teaching *and* singing. Our editorial staff, music stores, music publishers, and choir directors all over the country assisted us in collecting this rather complete listing of SATB octavos based on hymntunes found in *Hymns for the Family of God*. We found a number of hymntunes that have not been arranged in SATB format. Writers and arrangers who might be reading this should take note and fill this void with anthem material of high quality. There is a definite need! Dr. Fred Tulan, a world-renowned concert organist, church organist, organ teacher and clinician, and respected reviewer for *The American Organist* magazine, did an exhaustive amount of work in compiling what I feel is the handiest, most comprehensive and valuable of all organ guides. Church organists who know the validity of com-municating with their congregation through the playing of hymntune variations will rejoice over Fred's selections.

Section 5 is devoted to *Indexes*. Initially, you might want to skip over this section, but I request that you read on to see what we have included in these various listings. As we approached the index section of the hymnal, we made a decision to include only the minimal amount of indexes. The reason was that we felt the majority of hymnal users were not much interested in most of the material indexes contain. Instead, we put the bulk of the reference indexes into the *Companion*. Wanting to include as many selections in the hymnal as we could, the less space devoted to indexing, the more space we would be able to devote to hymns and Scripture and readings. All of the standard indexes found in most hymnals are included in this *Companion*—and then some! Our first index is a very special one: the first line of *every verse of every hymn*. Occasionally, an obscure line from an inner verse will come to mind: by using this index, you will easily be able to trace the location of that hymn. Second is the alphabetical index of hymntunes with metric division.

Next comes the metrical listing of hymntunes. An unusual feature of *Hymns for the Family of God* was the inclusion of last-verse descants and harmonizations right in the hymnal: the listing here is by title, by hymntune, and by category. John Seider, of Westmont College, has prepared a greatly expanded Scriptural Allusions in Hymns section which will be a welcome aid to those preparing services based on a specific Scripture verse, or those ministers who wish to support and enhance their sermons with hymn usage. Next is the alphabetical listing of all arrangers, authors, composers, sources, and translators—*anyone* who did *anything* that is included in *Hymns for the Family of God* is listed here with birth and death dates. Additional indexes include Collegiate Programs in Church Music (have a student interested in a career in Church Music? This listing gives 80 schools and universities to consider); a listing of Church Music conferences and workshops all over the country; suggested books and periodicals dealing with Church Music, Hymnology, and related subjects; a topical index (this is also found in the hymnal); and finally, a listing of names and addresses of all publishers and distributors who have materials listed anywhere in the *Companion*. I think you'll agree that we have indexed most everything under the Church Music sun. We might now be at the place where an index for the *Indexes* is necessary!

Clearly our purpose was to provide a companion book that presented a wide spectrum of views, ideas and comments on as many Church Music subjects as we could. It is our hope that this book be a useful one, one that will find continued and frequent use in the service of Him who gave us the words and the music in the first place.

FRED BOCK

The
Hymnal
Companion

I
Of Hymns and Hymnals

Prayer of Dedication

By William J. Gaither

Father, thank You for the gift of music. There are times when there is no other way to tell You that we are lonely, excited, happy, anxious, tired, or discouraged. Music is a beautiful way to express our deepest concerns, our thanks and our praise to You.

We thank You for the worship resources and Scriptures that are contained within this book. We pray that You will bless *Hymns for the Family of God* and the *Companion* to Your glory. We pray in Jesus' name.

Amen.

$\mathcal{A}$ History of Hymns and Their Use

By Howard Stevenson

THE SONG OF THE CHURCH—the body of believers, young and old, trained and untrained, professional people and laborers, home-makers and executives, ALL uniting in song to praise, to profess, to promise, and to pray. In spite of the justifiable importance given to the trained ensembles, congregational song remains the *most important song of the church*. We are never "one body" more than when we are engaged in this activity, especially in non-liturgical churches where the "work of the people" is minimal.

While modern technology helps us leap across great distances of space, to "be there" the instant world news is being made, the pages of our hymnal help us recapture something of King David's contrition, of Bernard's piety, of Luther's strength, of Wesley's doctrine, and Sankey's fervor. There is a new thrill every time we link hearts and voices with any one of these giants of our faith.

The Biblical foundations for the song of the church are laid in the largest book of the Bible, the Psalm-book, wherein Levitical choirs[1] in their antiphonal chants seem to vie with the people of Israel in their praise of God. The apostle Paul takes up the exhortation in Ephesians and Colossians: "let His words enrich your lives . . . sing them out in psalms and hymns and spiritual songs, singing TO THE LORD . . ." The Spirit of God has recorded some of the hymns of the early church in which they expressed their poetic cry for spiritual awakening (Eph. 5:14), or proclaimed their belief in the triune God (I Tim. 3:16).

The earliest hymns of the infant church were largely doctrinal and were used by Bishop Ambrose of Milan to combat the poison of the Arian heresy.[2] The music of these 4th century songs had no harmonies and might be compared favorably with the plainsong and chant we know

[1]Choirs composed of members of the Jewish tribe of Levi, which customarily supplied the music for the Jewish people.

[2]Belief that the Son is not of the same substance as the Father but was created as an agent for creating the world.

today. The alternation of long and short syllables helped parish members learn the text, and thus, the new coverts were strengthened against doctrinal error.

As the intricacies of the rules for conduct for liturgical services grew, congregational song disappeared from the *public* services. Nonetheless, a considerable number of fine Greek and Latin hymns have been passed down to us from the middle ages, the gift of such translators as John Mason Neale and Catherine Winkworth. These texts for private devotions combined with the Laudi Spirituali, the Latin folk music of the 11th century, made up a considerable body of hymnody that was extant when the reformers came upon the stage of history in the 16th century.

To Martin Luther belongs the distinction, as well as the gratitude of the church, for the restoration of congregational song to the laity. The reformer not only inherited Latin and German hymns of devotion hitherto used exclusively for private and family worship, but created new texts for the street songs as well as his own composed melodies. The German chorale left its mark for generations to come upon congregational song and the high art that was to flourish under the genius of such men as Buxtehude and Bach.

Although Martin Luther readily recognized the value of the art music of the Roman Church, his followers, the leaders of the Swiss and English movements, restricted their congregational singing to be exclusively that of the metrical psalms. After the persecutions of Queen Mary in England, Englishmen returned from Calvin's Switzerland to their homeland bringing the now-popular "Geneva-jigs" with them. Historians tell us that the rhythmic settings of the Psalms could be heard everywhere, sung by nobleman and merchant, soldier and commoner alike. All in all, some 326 metrical versions of the Psalms were produced. In fact, *Sternhold and Hopkins*, the most popular version, went through 200 editions and lasted for 10 generations in the established church as well as in the non-conforming congregations.

It remained for Isaac Watts in the first half of the 18th century to break the strangle-hold of the rhymed and metered psalms; he did it through paraphrasing and Anglicizing the songs of Israel. But by this, "eating their cake and yet able to have it, too," there was less resistance to the hymns of human composure. We hardly recognize the songs of David and Israel once Watts gets through with them, as evidenced in such "hymns" as *Joy to the World, O God, Our Help in Ages Past,* and *Jesus Shall Reign.* The work of the paraphraser became so popular and prolific that almost any modern day hymnal is sure to include a good portion of his work; something like the early American hymnbook of 1832 that ascribed 761 hymns to Watts out of a total of 1220 selections.

The Wesley brothers, John (1703-1791) and Charles (1707-1788), were only the first of a number of revivalists and evangelists who used hymnody to fan the fires of renewal they ignited in their home country. Although Charles was the hymn-writer, John saw to it as early as 1737 in Savannah, Georgia, that a hymnbook was made available for their parishoners. This was the first hymnbook ever used in an Anglican church. John and Charles' subsequent conversion in a Moravian meeting house started them on their life's work of reaching the masses of England's new industrial population. Stout doctrinal tenets were lifted from the pages of Scripture and sung in the fields, under the trees, and in the little congregations of uneducated men and women. Notice how the book of Romans shines through such a hymn as *And Can It Be*. Their sermons and their hymns quite literally changed the course of 18th century England, caught in the maelstrom of new industry, social evils, and oppressive clergy and politicians.

Then, as now, new life in the churches was borne along in new songs. The Welsh competed in hymn contests, Moody had his Sankey, and more recent pulpiteers such as Sunday and Graham are linked inseparably with their leaders of song: Homer Rodeheaver and Cliff Barrows.

In our own lifetime we have seen the coupling of new life and new song as the "Jesus people" incorporated their spontaneity and unsophisticated love for God and each other in hauntingly beautiful folk melodies and harmonies. Once again the church turned outside itself to find the kind of creativity that would be suitable for giving expression to new life. We owe a debt of gratitude to our young friends for loosing these wellsprings of joy that are so singable, simple, natural and accessible.

And yet, it behooves church musicians and leaders to examine the liabilities and possible pitfalls. It is increasingly difficult to define a body of literature—hymns or otherwise—that can safely be assumed to be known in any gathering of Christians. Our new young leadership has for the most part abandoned the great heritage of hymnody that has been referred to above. This fault should be avoided; we must not allow the limited contemporary texts to drive out the universal and timeless expressions of our Christian faith. The "mighty fortress" that sheltered and protected a German theologian is just as relevant in the 20th century as in the 1500's. If one turns solely to the output of the newer songs, one finds that these are constantly changing with new editions, new compositions appearing almost monthly. Much of the beauty and appeal of these "relational" songs deals with the "now" experience and subjectivity of the composer or the singer; they are not meant to take on a cloak of "immortality." Music leadership in the mid 20th century should maintain our great heritage of hymns on the one hand and yet be open to more recent songs of expression and experience on the other, recognizing the need and place of each.

Hymns for the Family of God reflects that philosophy in its eclectic choice of material, paying tribute to time-honored texts and melodies, and also making available the new "favorites" of today. Thus, there is available for every group of believers a wide choice of congregational songs to make up a total and diversified musical diet under one cover, and also to encourage involvement BY the people, rather than encouraging spectatorism, FOR the people.

One might inquire: where are the God-honoring and exalting hymns and texts of the 20th century . . . of the space age? They are, for the most part, still to be written. Perhaps some young author or composer reading these words will be the Watts or Wesley of our time, a person whose words or music will be sung in a 21st or 22nd century, if world history continues that long.

How then can we better exercise this privilege of congregational song? By esteeming this expression of God's people as something to be valued, understood, administered with thoughtfulness, and a uniquely qualified part of our "reasonable service." It is too easy to subject others, or to be subjected ourselves, to the routine, to the impersonal, and to the role of a spectator. Music has such tremendous potential for unifying, expressing, teaching, worshipping—or it can easily become "a narcotic to the soul." Erik Routley describes it thus: "no single influence in public worship can so surely condition a congregation to self-deception, to fugitive follies, to religious perversities, as thoughtlessly chosen hymns. The singing congregation is uncritical . . ."[3] Handle this hymnbook with care lest its promises, its prayers, its praises rise up to accuse you in a later day. The individual, the home, and the church will be rewarded with this kind of concern: For it is in blessing the Lord that we find our own blessedness.

Even in the 1970's and 80's, John Wesley's RULES FOR CONGREGA-TIONAL SINGING[4], written in 1770(?), are almost awesome in their insights:

1. Learn these tunes before you learn any others; afterwards learn as many as you please.
2. Sing them exactly as they are printed here, without altering or mending them at all; and if you have learned to sing them otherwise, unlearn it as soon as you can.

[3]Erick Routley. *Hymns Today and Tomorrow* (Nashville: Abdingdon Press, 1964) p. 22.
[4]John Wesley. *For Better Congregational Singing* (Dayton: Lorenz Industries, 1959) p. 4.

3. Sing ALL. See that you join with the congregation as frequently as you can. Let not a slight degree of weakness or weariness hinder you. If it is a cross to you, take it up and you will find it a blessing.

4. Sing LUSTILY, and with good courage. Beware of singing as if you were half-dead or half-asleep; but lift up your voice with strength. Be no more afraid of your voice now nor more ashamed of its being heard, than when you sing the song of Satan.

5. Sing MODESTLY. Do not bawl, so as to be heard above or distinct from the rest of the congregation—that you may not destroy the harmony—but strive to unite your voices together so as to make one clear melodious sound.

6. Sing IN TIME. Whatever time is sung, be sure to keep with it. Do not run before nor stay behind it; but attend close to the leading voices, and move therewith as exactly as you can; and take care not to sing too slow. This drawling way naturally steals on all who are lazy; and it is high time to drive it out from among us, and sing all our tunes just as quick as we did at first.

7. Above all, SING SPIRITUALLY. Have an eye to God in every word you sing. Aim at pleasing Him more than yourself or any other creature. In order to do this, attend strictly to the sense of what you sing, and see that your heart is not carried away with the sound, but offered to God continually; so shall your singing be such as the Lord would approve of here, and reward you when He cometh in clouds of heaven.

Thoughts on ©Copyright and the Copying of Copyrighted *Music*

By William G. Shorney

THE CHURCH MUSIC PUBLISHERS ASSOCIATION, founded some 50 years ago, represents a large and important group of publishers supplying music to the Christian church. One of its important responsibilities has been to disseminate information to leaders of church music programs. It is a privilege to be offered this space in order to inform church musicians of the provisions in the new copyright law of October 1976 that have particular application to their music ministry.

What Is Copyright?

Copyright is the exclusive legal right to make copies of intellectual property: books, music, poetry, pictures, drawings, etc.

Who Owns This Exclusive Legal Right To Make Copies?

The original creator(s); or assigned agents such as publishers.

Why Can't I Copy Anything I Want?

It's against the law to make unauthorized copies of copyrighted materials. It's something like dollar bills and postage stamps. You are not permitted to make your own.

Who Made This Copyright Law?

When the Founding Fathers wrote the U.S. Constitution, they empowered Congress to grant copyrights and patents to authors and inventors, for limited times, and Congress passed the necessary legislation.

What Was The Idea?

The Founding Fathers believed that a nation should stimulate and encourage its most creative people in order to promote the general welfare of ALL the people. The idea was to make the work of creative minds and hands directly profitable to the creators, by granting them an exclusive property right for limited times.

When Was The Copyright Law Most Recently Updated?

The most recent revision of the copyright law signed by the President October 19, 1976, went into effect on January 1, 1978. The law was originally written in 1909.

What Did the New Copyright Law Accomplish?

The recent revision of the copyright law must be regarded as a vast improvement over the earlier law as it updates the rights of authors and composers int he light of new technologies. It clarifies what musicians may do and what they may not do. It helps achieve a balance between creators and users.

What's This Business About "Limited Times"?

Copyrights and patents "run out" after a period of time. After the term expires, the intellectual property goes into the Public Domain, and becomes the property of all the people: anyone can then legally make copies.

How Can I Tell If A Piece of Music Is Copyrighted?

All copyrighted works bear a copyright notice in which the date of copyright is included. Under the old law, the term of copyright was 28 years with the possible renewal of an additional 28 years. However, during the legislative process leading to the new law, all copyrights from September 19, 1906, which had been renewed but which would other- wise have expired were extended so that they did not fall into public domain. Thus, all subsisting copyrights, if renewed, have a term of copyright of 75 years from the date copyright was originally secured. Therefore, to be safe, a church musician should assume that any publication which bears a copyright notice of 1906 or later is protected.

How Long Does The Copyright Term Run?

Musical works created after January 1, 1978, will be protected for the life of the composer (author) plus 50 years. Copyrights in effect on that date, if renewed, will continue for 75 years from the date copyright was originally secured. Those works in their initial 28 year period of copyright can be renewed for an additional 47 years, while the copyright of works presently in their renewal term are automatically extended for an additional 19 years. REMEMBER, any copyright prior to January 1, 1978, may continue for 75 years from the date copyright was originally secured.

Is Arranging Considered To Be Copying?

Yes. You must ask for and receive permission from the copyright owner before you are allowed to arrange a copyrighted piece of music.

What About The Words Only Of A Copyrighted Song?

If they are original lyrics, they are protected by the copyright, and they may not be copied without permission. This includes "song sheets." Texts from the Bible, Shakespeare, or any words written before 1906 are, of course, in the Public Domain and OK. Copyrighted texts from choir anthems, etc. are also protected and permission must be obtained for reprinting in church bulletins, etc. Also, copyrighted versions or paraphrases of Scripture are protected. Only the King James Version (KJV) is in the Public Domain.

Are There Any "Teeth" In The Copyright Law?

Yes. Under the present Copyright Law, people found guilty of violating the law are subject to fines and jail sentences. The law has been tested, and fines and jail sentences have been imposed by the courts.

What If I'm Faced With A Special Situation?

If you want to include copyrighted lyrics in a song sheet . . . or arrange a copyrighted popular song for a special musical group or occasion . . . or make any use of copyrighted music which the publisher cannot supply in regular published form, the magic word is: ASK. You may or may not receive permission, but when you use someone else's property—

intellectual or otherwise—you must have the property owner's permission.

What About Photocopies That Might Now Be In Our Performance Or Reference Library?

If the music is in its active copyright term, destroy any unauthorized photocopies immediately, and replace them with authorized legal editions. In effect, any illegal copies would put you in the position of harboring stolen goods.

What About The Photocopiers Who Don't Get Caught?

They are forcing the price of legal editions higher. They are enriching the manufacturers of copying machines at the expense of composers, authors, and publishers. They are risking embarrassment, at the least, from professional colleagues who understand the law; and they are risking fines and jail if they are taken to court.

What About Making A Custom Record Of Copyrighted Works By My Choir?

Permission must be obtained from the copyright holder. The maximum fee per copyrighted song is 2¾ cents which is set by law.

What About Transparencies Or Film Slides?

Transparencies and film slides may not be used for projecting copyrighted words or music without permission.

How Can I Get A Copy Of The New Law And More Information About It?

Write to:

> The Copyright Office
> Library of Congress
> Washington, DC 20559

II
Getting Ready to Worship God

The Minister Prepares

By Bryan Jeffery Leech

KEEP YOUR EAR TO THE GROUND. Pick up the candid responses of your people to the services of your church. Sift the feedback. You will notice that they refer to themselves as "the audience "and that they regard anything prior to the sermon as part of the "preliminaries"; so much so that, in many churches, people are still straggling in long after worship has begun. We who are ministers may deplore this state of indifference and passivity, but in large part we are responsible for it. For we have given the maximum amount of time to the preparation of the sermon, while at the same time treating all that goes before it and after it as if it were relatively insignificant; with the result that many an eleven o'clock hour resembles a four-course dinner in which a delectable main dish is preceeded by luke-warm soup, a wilted salad and followed by a tasteless dessert. Not for one moment do I wish to de-emphasize the importance of preaching, but surely our pulpit work would be enhanced if everything that surrounded it had the same freshness and creativity.

During my first fifteen years in the pastorate I used to spend anywhere from ten to fifteen hours a week on a message, and about twenty-minutes preparing the order of service and the other parts of a worship experience. I had a form sheet which listed an inflexible order of worship, and into this I inserted my choice of three hymns and the music chosen by the choir director and organist for their anthems, solos and preludes etc. But the sequence itself was as fixed as the law of the Medes and the Persians. Perhaps because my parishioners were used to it, they never seemed to complain about the dull sameness of this progression. Or was it that they were too kind to ever mention it?

I have heard of churches who take pride and comfort in the changelessness of their worship, who buck even the smallest alteration and feel a special security in knowing precisely when a given item in the bulletin will take place. They don't feel they've worshipped unless they've done so in a uniform motion that is inexorably the same. Obviously this fixed quality lies at the heart of the worship in churches

15

which use a prescribed liturgy, much of it filled with Scriptural content and matchless language. But in those traditions there is much more variety than is true in many of our free churches where, without such a resource, we slip into monotony and staleness without realizing it.

But for all those who applaud this indifference to change, there are others who sit in church chafing against the sameness or who, because they are creative people, look for a congregation that is willing to hoist its sail to the freshening winds of the Spirit. For if the Holy Spirit is anything, surely He is an exciting and creative presence. Yet somewhere along the line we must be quenching or grieving Him because so many of our gatherings are sterile and stale. Not only do we succeed in boring ourselves, but we are in danger of representing Christ to the non-Christian as someone who is tedious and old-fashioned, when in fact He is the most captivating and thrilling personality alive in our world today. No one has made this charge against us more tellingly than the late Dorothy L. Sayers, who wrote in her book, *Letters to a Post-Christian World*, "We have very efficiently pared the claws of the Lion of Judah, certified Him 'meek and mild' and recommended Him as a fitting household pet for pale curates and pious old ladies . . . He was emphatically not a dull man in His human lifetime, and if He was God, there can be nothing dull about God either." Having reminded us of the key events of Christ's life, death and resurrection she asks this question, "If this is dull, what, in heaven's name, is worthy to be called exciting?"

It is this very excitement which is missing from so many church services. And if it is to be restored, it must be found in those of us who lead worship. For undoubtedly the pastoral staff and the music ministers are the key to its restoration, especially the senior pastor. An obvious first step towards improvement is that of facing the challenge to make our worship more creative. From a practical standpoint just spending time praying about it; reading the many books on the subject; consulting hymnals, liturgies, magazine articles; all these can result in discovering a new channel for our creative energies. We must, of course, beware of anything that is theatrical and pretended. Nothing can be substitute for the genuine pulsating life of the Spirit inside us. Even so, ministers, because they are human, have their ups and downs, and they must lead worship in much the same spirit as the actor, who, when his heart is breaking, repeats the dictum that, "the show must go on." There have been many times in my own experience when, after a difficult Saturday in which some acute problem has arisen, I have faced Sunday morning with a dullness of soul and a physical tiredness that made me wish that someone else would take over. And, of course, someone else did take over. God took over. And He used the prayers and readings, the hymns and the order of worship which I had prepared when my mind was more at rest not only to bless the people but to bless me too. So, begin to expect God to work in and through all the parts of the worship experience, and prepare each part of it with meticulous care. The better prepared you are the more free you will be to make last-minute changes and to respond to the spontaneous promptings of the Holy Spirit.

Preparation is the key. Preparation of oneself. Preparation of all the various elements that constitute a service of worship. And in addition to the choosing of materials and people to be incorporated into it, there must be some degree of rehearsal. It may be argued that worship is not theater and that we must avoid the ostenatious and the artificial. I agree. But compare in your mind the self-conscious awkwardness of the wedding party at the rehearsal and the dignity and beauty of the ceremony itself and you will see that a run-through, rather than producing something that is false, provides those who are involved with the confidence to play their roles freely and naturally. Or, better still, attend the first reading of a play. Notice how awkwardly the actors say their lines. Words that should have power sound flat and meaningless because they are said without the sense and emotion they deserve. Then, go back on opening night. The performances have been honed to a fine edge. The dialogue crackles with life. The leading players seem not to be acting at all, they are so natural. And so it is with worship. When we know what we're doing and why we're doing it, when we've thought and prayed over every part of it, when we've endeavoured to find the best materials and the most gifted people for even the smallest details of the hour, even mundane things take on a significance they lacked before.

Very few things in life just happen. The best dinners, the most fun parties, the loveliest weddings all require hours of planning way in excess of the time it takes for the events themselves. A good meal is the result of careful marketing, the studious reviewing of cookbook and menu, skillful preparation and the imaginative setting of an elegant table. Equally important with the food to be served is the atmosphere of the room; and small touches; flowers, silver, linen, all serve to create an environment that enhances the meal. Part of hospitality is making your guests aware that you have gone to great pains to provide your best for your friends.

A few years ago I drove in the heat of summer to a large church in a rural area. I was well prepared for my part in the services; the sermon, the prayers, the music I was to perform had all been carefully chosen and worked through. Yet, there we were, ten minutes before the service was to start, with the minister calmly rifling through the hymnal choosing the pieces for congregational singing for that morning. Was I alone in finding the "preliminaries" meaningless? I am convinced that, as in anything else, our people only get out of a worship experience what we put into it.

I am not suggesting that the preparation of a particular service is the task of the minister all by himself. The ideal would be to have a Worship Nucleus made up of pastoral staff, the organist and choir director, and a number of creative people drawn from the congregation. It might be valuable to have one member whose assignment would be to search out innovative ideas; hymns, liturgies, prayers, formats, which could then be considered by the group for possible inclusion in various services of the church. Whereas the pastor must be the prime mover in this area, the creative gifts are seldom restricted to one individual however talented he may be. One of the ways to liven up public worship is to create ways for more people to be involved in it, both in the order of worship itself and in the behind-the-scenes planning beforehand. In churches where there are multiple services, sometimes as many as three in a single morning, there may be differences of style between the meetings, allowing for diversity of worship within a particular fellowship.

Obviously, all this takes time and many of us in the pastorate are pressured for lack of it. But surely the improving of worship must stand high on our list of priorities. For in that hour, each Sunday, we do more for more people at any one given time than during the rest of the week. We must make the most of this opportunity.

My own experience (having been to three excellent theological schools) is that, though we were trained to be excellent preachers, creative worship was scarcely thought of in those days. Happily, this is changing. The seminaries are aware of new trends in this area and are preparing ministerial students for parish ministries where the time-honored traditions are being challenged by new bursts of creativity among worship leaders and song writers. The great danger is that tradition becomes a mindless thing so that when we're questioned as to why a certain thing is always done in a certain way, we reply like Tevye, "I'll tell you . . . I don't know." We should, of course, hold on to everything good in our past. But it isn't necessary that the whole structure of worship be composed of antiques. New, fresh, modern ingredients placed alongside the old and the familiar can make the familiar things appear more worthwhile than ever before. Why shouldn't we move from a hymn in the chorale tradition to a simple chorus song to a Gaither piece? The church should use the best of all possible worlds, allowing the Holy Spirit to shine His light through the plate glass of this moment as well as through the stained glass of centuries past.

Some of us, in the Free Churches, need to get over our aversion toward set prayers. True, if they are repeated Sunday after Sunday they can become "vain repetitions," but so can some of our extemporaneous prayers when they are not well prepared. There is a great wealth of material to be mined from *The Book of Common Prayer* and other service books. If necessary, modernize the language where it seems obscure, but use the ideas of the collects and responses. Read the works of Michel Quoist and Leslie Brandt.* Read the Scriptures from different translations, choosing the best version of a particular passage. Provide your church with a first-rate hymnal or hymnal supplement, if you have more varied needs. Singing is so much a part of what we do together before the Lord that we owe it to our people to provide them with a collection of choice lyrics and music from many traditions, well arranged and clearly printed. It is because of this conviction of striving for excellence that *Hymns for the Family of God* was prepared as a worship book and not just a collection of hymns.

Some of us are gifted in the use of words. If you're a Peter Marshall of the Seventies you don't need this book, although it is interesting to note that the Chaplain to the United States Senate was not averse to using prayers written by other gifted writers. But if you lack spectacular inventiveness, cull ideas from others who have it and incorporate them into your ministry. We do this without apology when it comes to hymns, so why not borrow worship ideas, calls to worship, contemporary benedictions, and other elements which can brighten up your order of service? But be sure to ask permission if the material is copyrighted.

The turning point for me came when I was called to the Montecito Covenant Church adjacent to Westmont College in Santa Barbara. The church paid me the great compliment of appreciating anything I liked to try. They never said, "But we've never done it that way" and I shall never cease to thank them for the freedom this gave to me. We were without a choir during the major part of my pastorate, which challenged me to do something to compensate for this lack. Most of the orders of service printed in this book are composed from my stock of bulletins from those seven years. Necessity once again became the mother of invention, which leads me to believe that many of us are just not tapping our own inner resources and the gifts of the Spirit which the Lord desires to unearth among us.

Let me close with a word of caution and apology. You will have discovered that I have very decided opinions about what I like and dislike about church services. I have shared my feelings very frankly. I believe

*See Author Index to *Hymns for the Family of God*, p. 228.

too, that these standards of excellence can be achieved if we work for them. But having established the ideal, we must remember that we are shepherds of the flock and servants of the Lord's people. We have no right to come into a church and, overnight, force our tastes upon a group of people. We must start at the place where the congregation now stands. Our building of worship must take place slowly and gradually. We must win the right to be heard. We must gain the trust of the people. We must give them things they love and find familiar even if those things seem inferior to us, so that there are always parts of a service that reflect the church's tradition and which in turn buffer the shock of those parts of it that are startling and innovative. For what good will it do us if we achieve a perfect performance of worship and by so doing estrange half the people. On the other hand, any congregation worth its salt needs to trust its pastor with the same kind of confidence I received in Montecito. A man is bound to flourish under such supportive encouragement.

The Bible says little about worship. It says a great deal about God, the object of worship. This may indicate that no one style or way of worship is specially sacrosanct. God is more concerned with the heart than with the form. Nevertheless, the form that has depth and content can prompt the heart and lift the mind in a way that shallow material never can. It is our duty to provide the very best tools for today's worshippers. A sensitive pastor will know the right place for his flock. He will move them forward to grasses that taste sweeter, but he will do so so deftly that the sheep may not even be aware that they have left the old behind and are feeding on the new. Creativity must go hand-in-hand with sensitivity in accordance with the inner leading of the Lord. When this happens, Sunday by Sunday, there will be those who will whisper with gratitude,

"I was glad when they said unto me
Let us go into the house of the Lord."

The Music Minister Prepares

By Don G. Fontana

THE BEST WAY TO DEVELOP a relationship with a person is to spend time with that person. Worship is *spending time with God*. In considering the subject of worship we discover how best to prepare for worship; how to participate in worship and specifically, the meaning of worship.

Joseph Clokey, noted composer and church musician states in his book, *In Every Corner Sing,* "Worship is *honor* paid to God."[1] God is to be worshipped because He is *worthy* to be worshipped and to be praised. To worship requires effort. The worship experience can be infinitely more meaningful when we prepare ourselves to meet God. The goal in worship is to establish communication with God, to talk to Him, to listen, to wait, to learn, to concentrate, and meditate on God.

We can worship and communicate with God in many ways. Singing can be an act of worship. Praying, studying, waiting, listening, expecting —these are all integral parts of worship. We remind ourselves of the exhortation to "be still and know that I am God."[2]

Preparation for worship can be approached in three ways:
1. Thought
2. Prayer
3. Study

In *thought* we involve ourselves by concentrating on God. We take time for God to speak to us. He speaks through prayers, through Scripture, through hymns, and He speaks through daily experiences. We concentrate on clearing and cleansing our minds from thoughts unrelated to the worship of God. We acknowledge and review the many gifts God has given us, His children. We think specifically of the greatest gift of all—His Son, the Lord Jesus Christ. We think of the many other gifts in the form of forgiveness, compassion, love, watch-care, and eternal life to those who accept His Son into their lives.

[1] Joseph Clokey. *In Every Corner Sing,* 6th Ed. (New York: Morehouse—Gorham Co., 1975) p. 4. [Editor's note: unable to locate publisher as of 1979]
[2] Psalm 46:10

In preparing for worship we are able to have high levels of expectations from the experience of worship. We can look forward to having an encounter with the triune God: Father, Son and Holy Spirit. We can anticipate giving thanks to God, praising Him, confessing to Him, and enjoying a new experience of re-dedication of our lives, our talents and our energies. We look forward to receiving spiritual renewal. We share in the fellowship of other Christians and in the warmth and "family-ship" of the body of Christ, the Church. We remind ourselves once again that "God loves us" and that we love Him.

Another way we prepare for worship is through *prayer*. We pray for God's Holy Spirit to guide us and our thoughts, creating an openness to God's plan and purpose for our lives. We pray that God will place His ideas and His goals, for our lives, into our thoughts and dreams. We pray that God will speak to us through hymns, through Scripture, through special musical offerings and through the minister's witness. We pray that God will reveal to us the vast possibilities for our lives. We give thanks in our prayers, that we are in fact, a part of a family of God.

We pray for God to enable us to be used by Him, to be a blessing and an inspiration to others, allowing His love to shine through us. We ask for God to reveal Himself through our thoughts and through others. We pray for all who will lead in the worship service, that God will reveal Himself to each one. Our prayers may concern the request for special insight into specific personal needs. We request God's help in our own spiritual needs as well as those of others. We claim confidently that God will send His Holy Spirit into the worship experience.

Thirdly, we participate in *study*. Read Isaiah 6 and review the outline for worship. Here we see the *parts* of a worship service, their purpose and function. We discover the significance of praise and adoration. We learn the importance of confessing to Him things we need to tell Him. We discover the importance of giving ourselves in dedication and consecration for His use. Read or recall:

II Chronicles 5:13,14	John 3:16
Psalm 23	Romans 8:28
Proverbs 3:5,6	I Corinthians 13
Mark 9:23	Galatians 2:20
I John 1:9	Colossians 3:16

In some instances we are able to know the theme of the minister's message and thereby devote time to researching the subject. We can use the text of the hymns to be sung as a meaningful devotional resource in preparation for worship. Choir members can use the text of the anthem as an additional dimension to worship preparation. Use of the Scripture lesson and the responsive reading indicated will expand our understanding of the minister's message. We review all parts of the worship service as a framework for our personal encounter with God.

We look for related poetry or other writings by Christian authors to use in personal study. We look for published prayers that perhaps express the kinds of things that guide and prepare our thoughts and minds for a worship experience with our God. See selections # 329, 333, 340 and 364 in *Hymns for the Family of God*. We determine through our study that our purpose in worship will be that of an *active participant*. We will seek to give God reason to rejoice through our act of worship.

Finally, we read in II Chronicles 5:13, 14 that when the singers and instrumentalists were as one, it was at that moment God chose to inhabit His temple. So, sing my brother, sing my sister, play my instrumentalist friend and let it be together. For we await a guest, the greatest and grandest of all guests—our God, our Savior and our Friend. He enters His temple again, even NOW.

The Organist Prepares

By Fred Bock

WE READ IN II CHRONICLES 5:13 that the instrumentalists and singers were as one, united in their praise to God. Playing the organ for a service of worship demands this goal. It's easy, and quite natural, to want to draw attention to ourselves or what it is we're playing. (After all, we organists do spend a great deal of time learning notes, pedallings, fingerings, phrasings, and myriad of other details which are prerequisite to "good performance practice.") Concerts and recitals are the time for this kind of organ playing, a service of worship is *not*.

While there are ministers who feel what *they* have to say is the focal point of the service, and there are an equal number of choir directors who feel *their* contribution of anthems and solos are the featured event of the day, in truth, we are all worship *stagehands*—setting the stage, providing the scenery, and readying the background "props" to bring people closer to God. Oversimplification? I think not.

Having served in churches the past twenty years, one thing stands out—lots of people out there need a touch from God. To some, this relationship begins with the quietness of prayer, to some with the majesty of triumphant organ music, to some with the anthem or sermon of the morning. And to some, just being in the sanctuary after a week of fast-paced activities brings them a kind of solitude where they can catch their breath and renew their relationship with God. Worship starts with our getting in touch with God, and worship can come from many sources. Organists who think that God speaks only through the loud, difficult and demanding repertoire are in for a challenge from this writer! The communication ability of a simple hymntune arrangement can be as strong and winsome as anything on a Master's degree recital. The problem, as I see it, is that many organists lack *respect* for all styles of music. Few feel at home playing Baroque music *and* a romantic gospel hymn or quasi-rock folksong with the same energy, enthusiasm, dedication, and conviction. It takes more than flipping on the tremolo! Learning stylistics for various kinds of music so that each can be played *authenti-*

cally is a never-ending challenge. Making "The Old Rugged Cross" sound good on a tracker-action pipe organ takes some doing, but it *can* be done. By the same token, Baroque music *can* sound very good on a drawbar organ. *It can be done!*

As a balance to those statements, let me quickly add that there is a much greater problem: *selectivity*. As there is poor gospel music (few will argue that point), so there is also poor Baroque music, poor Classical music, and poor Contemporary organ music, too. The difficult task before us is to find *really good* organ music for service playing *from all eras*. *Variety* is the word to remember when it comes to selecting worship service music. Whatever you play this week, be sure that next week you play something entirely different. Try playing hymntune variations based on the opening hymn of the service. To this end, the Editors of this *Companion* enlisted the collative efforts of Dr. Fred Tulan. Fred's efforts are found in the *Index* section of this book. Many styles, composers, arrangers, and publishers are found in this listing of hymntune variations. All of the hymntunes are included in *Hymns for the Family of God*. When you play a hymntune variation, why not print a line in your bulletin that suggests to the congregation to follow the words as you play. This will make the piece more significant. (A suggestion to the organist: write in the words on your organ music, so that you have a sense of continuity and poetic phrasing as you play.

Much of the time, the organist accompanies. My favorite accompanying is playing for hymns. I start out with light registration: 8' and 4' Foundation stops, and gradually build each verse (playing word phrases, not just notes) until the very last verse resounds with full organ, mixtures, reeds, and on top of that, a keychange and reharmonization—*or both*!

Unusual use of registration is another area that can be made extra special. Whether you have a 5 manual/218 rank pipe organ, or a Thomas spinet, each has registrational strong points that should be utilized, and weak points that should be avoided. A major weakness of any organ is when it is played too loudly. On electronic organs, distortion can occur, and this certainly is not pleasant. Learn the instrument you have and dwell on its best resources. Don't get locked into three or four favorite registrations. Experiment with different sounds: try all sorts of registrations, with or without tremolo, played high, played low—be imaginative!

Another way in which the organist can help in preparing to worship God is to realize the importance of playing in the right spots, and *not* playing in others. It takes experience and a little know-how. Those interludes and organ responses need to be chosen with as much care as the prelude. A good example of a place when it is *right* to play is that awkward spot right after the opening hymn. People are being seated, hymnals are being replaced in the pew racks—and this is a time when the organ can "fill" and "cover" this activity. What often is done is to play the last four bars of the hymn softly. I don't mind the *softly* part, but why not use this occasion to play the hymn in a new key that will give a real lift to the service? A major third higher will do that. The abrupt change from E to Ab following "Holy, Holy, Holy," is a thrilling transition! (Eb to G is equally as nice for those who dislike playing in four sharps!)

Another subtlety that organists can add to a service is to play interludes or "fills" in preparation for the choir anthem or solo. It seems natural to play in the key of the solo or anthem. That creates a smooth segue and removes the jarringness of stop-start-stop-start.

Most of this article has been concerned with organists *preparing the congregation* for worship. I am concerned that most organists, because of their responsibilities in a service, rarely get to actually participate in worship themselves. This is unfortunate. Perhaps the thing that can draw us closer to God in worship is the knowledge that we are helping others meet Him through our playing. At the very least, we organists should pray before we play that our music will be honoring and pleasing to Him.

Prayer does not take the place of practice, nor does it take the place of hours spent searching for good usable music, nor does it take the place of rehearsing, transposing, reharmonizing, or registrating. But prayer, and a sincere desire to be used of God, make all of these efforts alive with the possibility that the organist can become a full-fledged Minister through Music.

Join me in this prayer:

Lord, help me as I work to make my organ playing something that You can use for Your glory. Remove from me any pride about my abilities. Be with me as I select even the smallest piece of music for the service. Guide me to choose the right one. Give me new and exciting ideas: help me to have variety and joy and majesty and a sense of mission in the music I play. Impress upon me a sense of ministering to my congregation, and help me to meet their musical needs and desires, but at the same time let me lovingly share with them the beauty of the music I hold dear.

And, having spent the necessary long hours of preparation, and having committed my playing to You, I pray that You will fill me with Your love; help me to play better than ever before, and reward my efforts with Your peace and joy in my life.

I play, and I pray . . . in Your name, and for the sake of bringing You closer to all who worship You!   Amen.

The Congregation Prepares

By Ray E. Robinson

PREPARATION FOR WORSHIP is directly related to one's attitude toward worship. Worship is not just one isolated element among many in the life of the believer, nor is it tied to any particular event in the life of the Christian. Rather, it is an attitude or orientation that should characterize the whole of it. Worship is not a theological blueprint drawn up by liturgical specialists who are considered leaders of worship, but an event, an encounter, if you please, between the Lord, Who through the Holy Spirit, acts in word and sacrament, and His people.

In Scriptural terms, the Christian's act of worship is one of presenting oneself a living sacrifice, in the words of the Apostle Paul, "holy, acceptable to God, which is your reasonable service." (Romans 12:1). The worship of the believer is thus a recognition of God's majesty and an acknowledgment of His sovereignty. Stated another way, it is reverential homage expressed in the adoration of and devotion to a personal God. To the Christian, true worship—whether corporate or individual—is one's willing response to the gracious invitation of the Creator God through His Son, Jesus Christ.

In the New Testament there is no essential distinction between worship and life: the believer's existence, for example, is not split into separate areas, one where Christ is honored and the other where the Christian operates more or less independently. Everything in the life of the believer stands under the Lordship of Christ. The true believer, therefore, must come to realize that worship embraces the totality of existence, not merely the more or less arbitrary hours which we set aside each week and call the Sunday morning service. Worship for the Christian is the center and circumference of life. In another Scriptural passage, Paul, the Apostle, reminds us of this thought: "Finally, brethren, whatever things are true, whatever things are honest, whatever things are just, whatever things are pure, whatever things are lovely, whatever things are of good report; if there be any virtue, and if there be any praise, think on these things." (Philippians 4:8).

What happens on Sunday, therefore, is not an isolated event in the life of the believer, but a particular facet of a perpetual experience, in company with others, and initiated in a desire to honor, praise and glorify the Creator God, and articulated through prayer, music, contemplation, and the hearing of the Word. If we really believe that worship is a perpetual activity, then our concept of the place of music in the service of worship will take on a new meaning. When considered in these terms, music becomes an act *of* worship, not merely preparation *for* worship. Nor does it become an art form that aids worship. When reduced to its most basic function in the regular corporate gathering of believers on Sunday, worship involves the communication of God's Word to His people and their response to it. The arts are no exception. Music is most effective in worship when it is conceived as a dialogue, initiating with the downward movement of the word in Revelation and following with the upward movement of the believer in response.

In true worship, then, there are no spectators, nor are there performers as such. Participation in worship is a natural response of every believer. It may come as a surprise to some church musicians to realize that the most important activity in the Sunday morning service is the involvement of the congregation. It is here that worship takes on a significant meaning for the individual believer. In the early Christian church, for example, the participation of laymen was assumed because there was no clergy. Corporate worship was conceived as a time when believers "thought and admonished one another in psalms, hymns and spiritual songs which were sung with grace in their hearts to the Lord." (Colossians 3:16, paraphrased). The participation of the individual was the key to a vital worship experience.

While this concept of worship, which places the primary focus on the congregation, and not on the so-called leaders of the corporate experience, seems to de-emphasize the role of the choir director, organist, choir and soloist, what it does in effect is free these musical specialists to prepare for and present a musical offering that is both unique and marked by unquestioned excellence.

Man is the unique creative act of God. He is created in God's image and every talent he possesses by virtue of this act exists to glorify the Godhead. The aesthetic life of the Church is therefore the beneficiary of man's God-instilled urge to respond in praise and devotion to a personal Creator. For the layman, it takes the form of a corporate expression, in company with others, and is articulated through prayer, contemplation and the hearing of the word. For the Church musician, it is an offering of the talent with which he or she is endowed, rightly related, rightly directed, and put to use in God's service. The implication here is clearly one of offering and stewardship: one's peers no longer become an audience in the corporate worship experience, as the primary concern of the believer becomes his or her relationship with Almighty God.

It is here that true preparation for worship takes place.

III

New Ideas for Exciting Services

Let's Be Creative

(some hints for adding new interest to worship)

By Bryan Jeffery Leech

CREATIVE WORSHIP must begin on our knees, with our minds centered on God. The Church is God's, not ours. We have been given temporary appointments as overseers of His people, that we may equip the saints for ministry. In most instances the pastor's involvement in a local congregation is comparatively brief in comparison to the career of that particular gathering of Christians. Our aim should be to always leave a church stronger than when we came. We shall accomplish that aim only when we realize our dependency upon God in all things, including our need to provide worship that is alive and glowing with the reality of His presence. Jesus once said, "According to your faith, be it unto you," and that still holds true. Any kind of renewal begins with faith and recommitment, which in turn is translated into the hard work of both immediate and long-range planning.

Let's assume that you are now determined to prepare well; that your church is beginning to build the necessary machinery for creative worship. Next Sunday is approaching. What do you do in order to plan an exciting morning for your people?

We can always assume that there are four basic needs which people have which should be met by any service of worship. There is the primary need of people to be reminded that they are creatures, that God is their Creator, and that they can only be fulfilled if they are filled full of Him. Then there is the need to be forgiven. Everyone drags around with some burden of guilt. It may be conscious or unconscious, but it is there nonetheless. Thus we need to be reminded, every time we come to church, that God loves us as we are, that he wants to lift this weight from our hearts and, by His love, inspire us to live lives that avoid sin as much as possible. It can also be assumed that in every group of people there are those who need to be comforted. Behind many a bright face there is a heart close to breaking; the order of service should always say something that heals and helps such battered folk and gives them strength to face the gale-force winds through which they may be struggling. Equally important is the need we all have to be prayed for and to pray for others. We come out of a society that is tending to overstress our individuality, which advises us "to do our own thing" often without regard to its effect on others. In church we receive a completely opposite directive which reminds us that we are "family" with all the other disciples of Jesus, and that they are there to support us and we are there to support them. So, adoration and thanksgiving, supplication and intercession, confession and comfort must be woven into the fabric of worship.

Each emphasis can be brought in in a number of ways. For example, the element of comfort could be stressed in a reassuring Call to Worship, in a hymn such as "O God, Our Help in Ages Past," in one of the lessons, in the pastoral prayer, in a solo or anthem, even in the announcements, when in sharing that the congregation is caring for a sick person, someone who is worried about what would happen if he or she were to become ill is reminded of the authentic love manifest in pastor and people alike. The sermon, of course, meets a further need, the need of Christians to have the Word of God explained and to be made aware of divine marching orders for the next stage of life.

Having established the major ingredients we want to include, it may be helpful to build a particular service around a central theme. It might be "guidance" or "forgiveness" or "resurrection" or some other seasonal observance in the church year. In most instances it will correspond with the subject to be dealt with in the sermon, so that when the minister begins to preach the congregation has already spent half-an-hour considering his topic. Thus it becomes necessary to select hymns, prayers, readings, solos, anthems, etc., which enhance and underscore the main thrust of the hour.

Here are some of the ingredients that can be incorporated in the ways we have suggested:

Praise
Thanksgiving
Comfort
Sharing
Informal Prayer—sentence prayers
Challenge—sharing of concerns, needs, etc.
Music—by soloists, choirs, groups
Instrumental music—organ, piano, violin, orchestra
Liturgy, litany, set-prayers, responses, readings
Sacraments—baptism, communion
Dedication—of children, missionaries, staff people, buildings
Special events—summer schools, seminars, guest preachers, series
   films, dramas, skits

Announcements—by laymen as well as the pastoral staff
Offerings
Recognition of key personnel
Welcoming visitors
Receiving new members
Children's sermons, services conducted by young people
Children's hymns
Decorations—flowers, banners, art, candles, dance, symbolism, bulletins
Sermon—dialogue, messages in two parts, monologues, dramatic readings, modern parables
Cantatas, extended anthems
Special events—graduation, confirmation
Layman's Sunday
Pulpit Exchange Sunday
Denominational Observances
Missions Conference
Lord's Prayer, Pastoral Prayer, Invocation
Testimony
Weddings

Once you have decided on the core idea, assemble the various elements around it. If you can block out your preaching-plan weeks and even months ahead, you then allow for the added advantage of giving your committee plenty of time to research suitable material for a particular service. It is very important that the senior pastor and the minister of music have complete control over what is done. Unfortunately, in many churches, soloists tend to choose their selections without conferring with the worship leaders. This can lead to the inclusion of material which, textually, is of inferior quality and unsuitable for a gathering of Christians. It should be pointed out to anyone aspiring to sing in church that this kind of control is essential. The Minister of Music may handle the problem either by asking the singer to submit a number of possible songs, or by recommending more suitable material and offering to coach the soloist in learning this new music. We must always hold in mind that our purpose in using music in the church is primarily that of conveying ideas through a sacred text (which must be theologically correct and reverent in feeling) and, to a lesser degree, that of creating a suitable mood for a meeting with God.

It would seem most desirable that the Minister and Choir Director should choose the hymns together. Where possible there should be a balance between familiar songs and new material. The latter should be introduced gradually, with the organist using a new song as interlude music, or with the choir singing an anthem based on a particular hymn. Many hymns are now arranged in choral settings, and a list of these is provided, beginning on page 98.

Some congregations have a "Hymn of the Month" as a means of expanding the repertoire of the congregation. It is especially important that the hymn following the sermon be one that underscores the message, so that it serves to drive home the central idea of the entire service. This means that the Minister and the Minister of Music need to familiarize themselves with the hymnal. A good way to do this is to use it at home and to treat it as a devotional supplement in one's own prayer life. It is also vital that a record be kept of the hymns used so that overuse on the one hand and neglect on the other are avoided.

We speak a great deal of "sacred music" but there is really no such thing; for any good tune set to sacred words could also be matched with a fine, secular lyric. To most Christians the *Maori* tune brings "Search me O God" immediately to mind, but many of us who lived through the late 40's find the memory stirring of Gracie Fields singing, "Now is the Hour." The melody no more belongs to one set of words than to the other, but it suits both texts because it enhances a lovely spiritual song as well as a fine romantic ballad. Thus music only really becomes sacred when it supports words which in turn remind us of God. It is possible to sing the Doxology to "Hernando's Hideaway" but a tango rhythm seems out of place in a solemn service of worship. But having said this, one notices that melodies and rhythms, instruments, and vocal styles which once were tabu have come into the church, which simply illustrates that even in the Church tastes do change. The important question is this, does the music suit the text in question? A prayer to the Holy Spirit should not be boisterous and a challenge to risk one's life for God should not be calm and subdued. It would have been unthinkable for Arthur Sullivan to have composed "Onward Christian Soldiers" to a waltz rhythm, because soldiers march, they do not dance. The greatest music, for example Stainer's "God so Loved the World," #20, perfectly reflects the feeling of the lyric. A quite opposite illustration would be the Gaithers' "Get All Excited," #652, which pulsates with rythmic feeling in keeping with the enthusiasm of the words. Sometimes interesting things can result from a re-matching of a text with a new tune. In Europe many hymnals have only the printed lyrics and the choice of melody is left to the choir master. (See the metrical index, page 183.)

An opposite problem from that of learning new music is that of overusing things that are familiar. Some songs become too popular. We know them so well that their message no longer reaches us, and it becomes difficult for us to "sing with understanding" and to concentrate on what is being said. Thus it may be wise to avoid using certain pieces for a while or to sing the well-worn words to a fresh melody. For example, "My Hope is Built on Nothing Less" fits very well in the tune *Melita*, most familiar to us as "The Navy Hymn."

Perhaps the most exciting thing about the evangelical church of today is its openness to music of all styles and origins. The climate for fresh creativity has never been more favorable than it is today. The Catholic Church is discovering the wealth of Protestant hymnody while Protestants sing "They'll Know We are Christians by Our Love" without always realizing its beginnings in the Catholic communion. Hymnals have *always* been ecumenical, long before the term was invented, but they have never been so broadminded as they are today. It is a humbling thing for us to realize that God has His people in every time in every place and that no one has a complete monopoly on the truth. New hymns sprout up into the sunshine in the most unlikely places, just as flowers bloom in bogs as well as in formal gardens and are no less fragrant than the more cultivated variety. It has been our aim, in assembling this collection of songs and worship aids, to choose the best of each type, ranging from the grand, objective, classic hymns of the Faith to some of the newer and more relational compositions of the last few years. Compared with several recently published hymnals, we have included a greater amount of new pieces, many of them written by younger writers.

Our book, *Hymns for the Family of God*, is now in your hands. We have done our best to bring it to you. Take it and use it well to the glory of God. That's all we ask, for who can ask more?

*c*All on a Sunday *c*Morning

Announcements

Each church has its tradition about the announcements. It is a shame that we have to have them at all, that we can't assume that people will read the bulletin and leave it at that. But since we seem compelled to have them, they should be given in such a way that they interrupt the mood and flow of the service as little as possible. The best time to have them is at the beginning of worship immediately after the congregation has been welcomed and before worship proper has commenced. The least desirable time, in my opinion, is at the conclusion to the service. I am thinking of the fact that they can so easily break the mood created by the service and the message, and cause people to forget the serious resolves they may have made in the presence of the Lord. Most churches place them in the middle of the hour, immediately before the receiving of the offering. This tends to dissect the worship experience and also to link the important moment of surrendering tangible gifts to God with events that are sometimes rather mundane and trivial, which may be why so many of us fail to see the offering as a vital part of worship.

Having conceded that we must have them, here's a suggestion that someone other than the pastor be the one to give them. If you've noticed the newscasters on television, the same person seldom talks for very long at one time. There are teams of newscasters. One man gives the weather, another the local news, another items of national and international importance. Yet in our services the senior pastor tends to do everything. This is one job that he could easily delegate to a man or woman with an outgoing personality and good diction, (who can also be bothered with those irritating last-minute changes that come in during the count-down before 11 a.m.)

Scripture Reading

It is the custom in the Church of England that the two lessons, one from the Old Testament, one from the New, be read by a member of the congregation. Why not try this in your church?

Of course, the reader must be selected carefully. Details of the passages for a given Sunday should be sent to him in sufficient time so that he is thoroughly familiar with them, and can read them with accuracy and imagination. Older children should be included on the roster for such readings, especially on Sundays when there is a particular emphasis on youth. We have provided a hundred readings in *Hymns for the Family of God* from nine different translations. They were chosen because of their suitability for being read aloud.

Decorations

In many churches there seems to be an unwritten law which states, "When you come to church, leave your eyes at home." Audibly there may be much upon which to feast; the written word, the spoken word, music, singing, instruments, and in a few churches very elaborate architecture to create its own sense of mystery. But apart from the magnificence and beauty of the edifice itself and the visual splendor of the flowers on the altar, there is little for the eye to behold that it has not seen on a previous Sunday. The danger of the most inspired architecture is that after a while it becomes usual and commonplace.

In recent years there seems to have been a renaissance of art within the church. We seem to be discovering people with the skills to portray the faith in visual terms. Painters and sculptors are beginning to remind us of the symbols of our Christian heritage through banners and mobiles and paintings. Two years ago, at Pentecost, I visited a church in Pasadena, California. Above the chancel was a plain wooden cross. Suspended above it, as if floating in air, was a flock of doves made of white paper and attached to one another at the wing-tips. It gave the worshipper a splendid and unforgettable visualization of what the season means which commemorates the giving of the Comforter to the early church. At Easter, the following year, a banner was thrown across the same cross; made of some rough material it bore the words, in blood red, "He is risen." That splash of crimson with those thrilling words is something I shall always remember.

Bulletin covers offer marvellous opportunities for the use of creative talent. On a much larger scale, we can do so much to encourage creative people by establishing an annual art festival. In many congregations, and in some para-church organizations such as "The Lamb's Players" and "The Covenant Players," drama is being recognized as a most effective means both for evangelism and for teaching.

Prayers

It is a solemn responsibility to pray for other people. It requires the same careful thought and prayer as delivering a sermon. One needs to ask oneself each week, "Where are my people at this particular moment in time?" Personally, I have found it helpful to write out all my prayers even if I abandon the paper when I come to deliver the prayer in the actual service. The reason for writing it out word-for-word is that most of us develop habits in which we overuse idioms and overwork phrases. We can slip into "vain repetition" without realizing it unless we have it there before us. Some of us who pride ourselves on our spontaneity are the worst offenders. I like the story of the minister in England who prayed every Sunday that the Lord would "sweep away the cobwebs of sin." His parishioners soon became fatigued by the excessive use of this metaphor, until one day a courageous elder prayed," Lord, for goodness sake, kill that spider." When we write out our prayers we objectify them; we can see where we overstress one theme and neglect another. We can notice any tendency to become obscure, to use the language of Canaan, to use a cumbersome word when a simple term would be quite adequate. We can develop language that will take a common thought and make it extraordinary, when we take the time; but few of us are so gifted that just the right word comes as soon as the idea forms in our minds. The popularity of the Book of Common Prayer, the liturgy of the Lutheran Church, and the traditions of many ancient communions is as much due to their superlative way of stating a truth as to the correctness of the theology those liturgies contain. Who can describe sin more accurately than to say, "We have left undone those things which we ought to have done, and we have done those things which we ought not to have done." Sin is both omission and commission and the Prayer Book defines it perfectly.

Ideally, our prayers should receive as much careful preparation as our sermons, for they are the means by which we lead our people into the presence of God and are just as important as those words which we bring them as a message from God.

Congregational Involvement.

As we saw earlier, many congregations are referred to and treated as "an audience." Worship is not dissimilar to a play, a concert, a film. Arriving at the proper place at the appointed time, the worshipper settles himself down in his pew and waits for others to conduct him through the morning's routine of devotion. His role, in many churches, is almost entirely passive. This is regrettable, because it has been proved beyond a doubt that we gain the most benefit from those things that we do rather than from those things that we merely spectate. Apart from singing an occasional hymn and placing money in the offering plate, the average congregation observes when it should participate. The very fact of having an order of worship that is uniquely different from last Sunday's alerts the congregation and compels it to pay attention.

But we must get away from this mistaken notion of God's people gathering to watch a religious drama. If anyone is the audience it is God. He has promised to be there, where two or three are gathered in His name. All of us are to play a role in what amounts to a benefit performance for and to God. We come together to offer up our praises to Him. The ministers may be the chief actors, but they play their parts only to inspire us to follow them. Indeed, it might be more accurate to say that they are the directors, showing us what we can do to tell God of His greatness, and reminding us, through their preaching, what the script really says and what the next act in the play will reveal.

To change our metaphor to one of sports, we must get the people off the bleachers, down on to the field. The pastors may be playing-coaches, but they are not the team and cannot play the game by themselves. Thus anything which will involve the mass of the people, anything which will convince them that the worship belongs to them, is to be welcomed. Some of the most inspiring prayers I have ever heard were given by a Japanese-American who runs a nursery. His pastor recognizes his gift and allows him full use of it. Many laymen have a gift for preaching and can add great richness to the life of the church if their pastor will appreciate their talent. How wonderful it is when a congregation is the first to recognize the emergence of a young person with gifts for ministry by giving him or her the chance to witness to that gift. My home church has encouraged and helped to develop a young man with remarkable abilities in evangelism. He may owe his entire career, humanly speaking, to their initial awareness of his potential.

Worship is something we can only do in community. We can worship God in private, in isolation, but we are commanded to "assemble ourselves together," for the New Testament knows nothing of solitary religion. The ideal fellowship is one led by pastors, by trained personnel, where the gifts of each member are developed and used for the common good. Like a good orchestral conductor, the pastor educates his players; teaches each of them his part in the score; and then inspires them to play, not solos that sound above the rest, but a sensitive performance that has an ear to the others and an eye fixed resolutely on his baton and the music itself. He creates what is called a sense of ensemble, where all the gifts merge into a glorious whole.

Advent Ideas

Prelude

Welcome and Announcements

Choral Introit #166 Let All Mortal Flesh Keep Silence

Prayer

Lighting of the Advent Candle

Opening Hymn of Praise and Readings
   Hymn #169 O come, O come Emmanuel
                And ransom captive Israel
                That mourns in lonely exile here
                Until the Son of God appear.
                Rejoice, rejoice, Emmanuel shall come to thee,
                O Israel.

   Reading Isaiah 11:1-3
   Hymn   O come, Thou Day-spring, come and cheer
                Our spirits by Thine advent here;
                Disperse the gloomy clouds of night,
                And death's dark shadows put to flight.
                Rejoice, rejoice, etc.

   Reading Isaiah 11:4-5
   Hymn   O come, Thou Wisdom from on high,
                And to order all things, far and nigh;
                To us the path of knowledge show,
                And cause us in her ways to go.
                Rejoice, rejoice, etc.

   Reading Isaiah 11:6-11
   Hymn   O come, desire of nations, bind
                In one the hearts of all mankind;
                Bid Thou our sad divisions cease,
                And be Thyself our King of peace.
                Rejoice, rejoice, etc.

Scripture Lesson #165 Beginning (John 1:1-14)

Choir Anthem #168 Come, Thou Long-Expected Jesus

Offering and Offertory

Doxology

Solo #174 Lo! How a Rose E'er Blooming

Unison Reading #176 The Magnificat

Hymn #210 I Cannot Tell

The Sermon

Hymn #170 Thou Didst Leave Thy Throne

The Lord's Prayer

The Blessing (said to one another)
> The Lord give you light
> > as you prepare to celebrate His birthday;
> > as you prepare to be generous to others;
> > as you send greetings to relations and friends;
> > > that you may have the grace to make your own
> > > > traditions fresh and alive with new meaning.
> Leader: The Lord loves you, everyone.
> > The Lord is with you, everywhere.
> > The Lord provides for you, everything.
> > Rejoice and be at peace. Amen.

Postlude #172 Of the Father's Love Begotten

ADVENT WREATH

The tradition of lighting an Advent wreath is practiced in many churches and is especially beautiful when it is done by members of the congregation. A family may be appointed to light a candle on each of the Sundays of Advent, with the Father reading a brief explanation of the ceremony while one of the children does the actual lighting. Or it can be done by Fathers and sons, or Mothers and daughters.

The season of Advent is a very useful time in the life of the Church, especially because of the tendency for Christmas to become commercialized. It is a way of reminding the people of God to get their priorities in order and to make worship the center of the holiday season.

Christmas Ideas

Meditation #189 How Proper It Is

Prelude #180 What Child is This?

Processional Hymn #179 The First Noel

Lighting the Advent Candle

Opening Hymn #193 O Come, All Ye Faithful

Call to Worship
Leader: Good morning. A joyous Christmas to you!
People: Good morning. This is one of the great days of the year, for it is
      a reminder of gloriously good news.
Leader: What is the good news we recall and the reason for our
      celebration?
People: The good news is this, that God has entered human life.
      "For unto us a Child is born,
      unto us a Son is given."
Leader: Let us think again of the wonder of this great fact of history,
      of how Christ emptied Himself,
      sharing first our life, and then our death,
      and who conquered death by rising again.
All: We praise Him who came in simplicity long ago and who will
      come in splendor very soon. Amen.

Hymn #177 Good Christian Men, Rejoice

Prayer #188 Christmas

Choir Anthem #190 Angels from the Realms of Glory

Unison Reading #191 Luke 1:68-79

Solo #198 Child in the Manger

Prophecies of His Coming Isaiah 9:6-7; Luke 1:26-33

Pastoral Prayer & Lord's Prayer

Sermon Scripture

Solo #201 The Star Carol

Preparation for giving #200 His Love . . . Reaching

Offering and Offertory

Doxology

Prayer

The Sermon

Closing Hymn #184 Hark! the Herald Angels Sing.

Benediction

Postlude #171 Joy to the World!

A Service of Worship for Palm Sunday

Prelude #376 Glorious Things of Thee are Spoken

Choral Introit #379 Bless His Holy Name

Call to Worship
> Leader: For a moment let's just forget ourselves and think only of God.
> People: We think of the Father,
> > all-knowing, all-powerful,
> > ever-present in all places,
> > always holy,
> > always loving,
> > always providing.
> > We think of Jesus Christ;
> > living a perfect life;
> > dying a sinner's death;
> > alive again and about to return.
> > We think of the Holy Spirit;
> > who lives in us,
> > prays for us,
> > works through us,
> > and creates unity among us.
> Leader: In our better moments we realize that nothing matters except God and our duty to Him.

Hymn #249 All Glory, Laud and Honor

Responsive Reading #243 Who is This Man?

Prayer of Praise and Thanksgiving

Anthem #320 Let Us Celebrate the Glories of our Lord

Announcements & Offering
> Leader: Before we participate in this offering this morning, I want to ask you these questions: What recent proofs have you given of your love for Christ? Have you ever done something for Him that really cost you something? Remember, the giving Jesus commended was that which was sacrificial.

Doxology (Sung to tune #347)

Prayer (unison)
Lord, help us to prepare ourselves to celebrate this year's Easter; by spending more time thinking through this, the greatest event in history; in the renewing of broken promises; in fervent prayer for those who will be celebrating with us; in concern for those who may be awakened to faith as they hear the Easter message; and in the sacrificial giving of ourselves to those who may need us during this very special week. Through Christ our Lord, we pray. Amen.

Pastoral Prayer

Hymn #625 Lord, Speak to Me .

The Sermon

Closing Hymn #248 Hosanna, Loud Hosanna

Benediction

Postlude #336 O Worship the King

A Service of *Holy* Communion

Prelude #115 There's a Wideness in God's Mercy

Announcements and Welcome

Choral Introit #104 Great God of Wonders

Call to Worship #388 His Love is Everlasting

Opening Hymn #387 We Gather Together

Invocation

Thanksgiving #396 A General Thanksgiving

Old Testament Lesson #23 Hosea 14:4b-9

Pastoral Prayer
  (concluding with The Lord's Prayer)

New Testament Lesson #280 Romans 5:1-11

Anthem #277 Jesus, Priceless Treasure

Meditation "The Meaning of Holy Communion"

Prayer

Hymn #428 Come, Ye Sinners, Poor and Needy

The Service of Holy Communion

Prayer of Confession (unison)
  All-powerful and forgiving God,
  We have wandered away from You,
  not like children who innocently lose their way,
  but like sheep who willfully follow anyone who will
  lead them, without caring which direction they take.
  We've pursued our own wills and desires;
  We've trusted our own judgment instead of the truth of your Word;
  And by so doing we've countermanded many of your rules for living.
  Lord, don't disown us for what we've done, but draw us
  closer to Yourself by another act of loving forgiveness. Amen.

The Lord's Supper

Distribution of the Elements

Silent Prayer

The Blessing (said in unison)
   "Worthy is the Lamb that was slain, to receive power, and wealth and wisdom, and might, and honor, and glory and blessings. To Him who sits upon the throne and to the Lamb be blessing and honor and glory and might, forever and ever. Amen." (Revelation 5:12)

Offering and Offertory

Benediction

Postlude #238 Jesus Shall Reign

Easter Ideas

Prelude #288 Jesus Lives, and So Shall I

Welcome and Announcements

Call to Worship
    Leader: Christ is risen! He is the Victor!
    People: He is risen, He is risen indeed!
    Leader: He lived and died in past history.
    People: He lives and influences present history.
    Leader: He promises to be here with us where two or three are gathered in His name.
    People: We celebrate His triumph. We recognize His presence. We applaud His achievements. We declare our love for Him in this act of worship. Amen.

Processional Hymn #289 Christ the Lord is Risen Today.

Prayer #294 Easter

Anthem #301 Easter Song

Unison Reading #290 I Corinthians 15:12-28

Solo #295 I Know that My Redeemer Lives

Prayer
    Leader: When we look at our world and its troubled condition;
           When we see the vast majority of people indifferent to You;
           When we sense the pessimism and hopelessness of the atmosphere about us;
           When we're tempted to relax our standards and to be no different from the world about us:
    People: Father, remind us then that Christ is the Victor, that He is alive, and that He is coming again.
    Leader: When we're tried beyond our strength;
           When we're caught in a web of suspense;
           When we must stand by and see someone we love suffer;
           When we're sorely tempted by that sin which besets us;
           When we're most conscious of our frailty and weakness;

People: Father, remind us then that Christ is the Victor, that He is alive, and that He is coming again.

Leader: When we've tried to explain You to someone we love, without apparent response on their part;
When our prayers seem to be unanswered;
When our labors bring no apparent results;
When our actions are misinterpreted;
When we dare to be different and are condemned for shaking the status quo and for speaking the truth in love:

People: Father, remind us again that Christ is alive, that He is always with us when we stand for Him, and that there are great rewards for such loyalty. Help us to live each day in the joyous awareness that He is alive and involved in all that we do. He is risen! Amen.

Sermon Scripture

Offering and Offertory

The Doxology

Hymn #298 Christ Arose

The Sermon

Closing Hymn #292 Because He Lives

Benediction

Postlude

Pentecost Sunday Service

(7th Sunday after Easter)

Prelude (A time of preparation for worship)

Welcome and Announcements

Choral Introit #155 Spirit of the Living God
#146 The Holy Spirit

Hymn #159 There's a Sweet, Sweet Spirit in This Place

First Lesson #158 Joel 3:1-5

Opening Prayer

Second Lesson #156 I Corinthians 2:10-16

Prayer (in unison)
"Almighty God, unto whom all hearts are open, all desires known and from whom no secrets are hid; cleanse the thoughts of our hearts by the inspiration of thy Holy Spirit, that we may perfectly love Thee and worthily magnify Thy holy name; through Jesus Christ our Lord. Amen."*

Choir Anthem #147 Spirit of God, Descend Upon My Heart

Pastoral Prayer

The Lord's Prayer #440 sung in unison

Offering and Offertory

The Doxology #382 Praise God, from Whom All Blessings flow

Hymn #162 Holy Ghost, with Light Divine

The Sermon

Hymn #151 Spirit, Now Live in Me

Response #160 Give us Your Holy Spirit

The Blessing May you go with God, and God will go with you.
May I go with God, and God will go with me.
May we both go with God and we shall walk in unity and peace with one another. Amen.

*From "The Book of Common Prayer." Used by permission of Charles Mortimer Guilbert as custodial of The Standard Book of Common Prayer.

Thanksgiving

Prelude #385 Holy God, We Praise Thy Name

Call to Worship
  Minister: O give thanks to the Lord, for He is good, for His steadfast
      love endures forever. (Psalm 136:1)

Choral Introit: #387 We Gather Together

General Thanksgiving #396

Hymn #395 We Plow the Fields and Scatter

A Litany of Thanksgiving
  Leader: For what You are to us, Oh God,
          Creator, sustainer of our world
            and all things in it;
          Savior, Redeemer of all men who believe
            and are sensitive to the inner witness;
          To You, Father, Son and Holy Spirit. . . .
  People: We give You the thanksgiving of our hearts,
          the praise of our lips
          and the service of our lives.
  Leader: For the beauty and wonder of our world;
          For the richness and suitability of our natural environment;
          For the unlocked secrets of nature which make life
            comfortable and healthy and pleasing.
          For the arts and sciences; for all things that
            inform the mind, bring health to the body
            and enrich our common life. . . .
  People: We give You the thanksgiving of our hearts,
          The praise of our lips
          And the service of our lives.

Hymn #389 Let All Things Now Living

Litany
  Leader: For our country and its magnificent past;
          For the liberties and rights of each individual;
          For the opportunities of self-development
            and education granted to our most ordinary
            citizens;

53

For growth of understanding between the races;
For those whose roots reach back to the beginnings
of our history
And for those whose accents speak of
foreign birth and recent arrival.

People: We give You the thanksgiving of our hearts,
The praise of our lips
And the service of our lives.

Leader: For the religious heritage which formed our earliest way of
life:
For the tolerance that has been a part of our history;
For the faithful in prior generations who carried forward
the torch of truth, preaching the gospel at the point
of personal sacrifice;
For seasons of revival which shaped churches and gave birth
to fresh expressions of faith;
For great men remembered and faithful men
forgotten, all of whom added spice to the flavor
of the Church as it has come down to us.

People: We give You the thanksgiving of our hearts,
the praise of our lips
and the service of our lives.

Leader: For our salvation, initiated by the Father's love and ac-
complished
by the Son's obedience and made real to us through
the witness of the Spirit;
For the removal of guilt when we have sinned, for the
surmounting
of sin when we have resisted temptation, and for the
direction of our lives by the Holy Spirit.
For this fellowship whose people bring their gifts to us and
who, by their love, create the warmth in which our gifts can
flourish:
For our homes; for wives and husbands, grandparents, sons,
daughters, uncles, aunts and cousins and all those special
people who seem to be of our blood because, in Christ, we
are one with them. . . .

People: We give You the thanksgiving of our hearts,
The praise of our lips
And the service of our lives.

Hymn #392 Come, Ye Thankful People, Come.

Scripture Lesson #388 His Love is Everlasting
  (Psalm 126:1-9, 16-18)

Offering and Offertory #394 Rejoice, Ye Pure in Heart

Prayer #391 Thanksgiving Day

Anthem/Solo #390 O, Let Your Soul Now be Filled with Gladness

The Sermon

Hymn #525 Now Thank We All Our God

Benediction

Postlude #520 Lord, Dismiss Us with Your Blessing

Morning Worship Service with Holy Communion

Prelude #276 Come to Calvary's Holy Mountain

Hymn #283 What Wondrous Love is This?

Call to Worship
    Leader: God is with us.
    People: He is indeed.
    Leader: How do we know this to be true?
    People: By His promise that where two or three are gathered in His
             name, He is there among them.
    Leader: God's Word assures us of His presence,
             His Spirit confirms His presence.
             Now, by your own faith and love for the Lord.
             join in this love feast and celebration of
             Holy Communion.
    People: In so doing we remember that He died for us.
             In so doing we anticipate His coming again.
    Leader: God is with us.
    People: He is indeed.

Prayer

Anthem #284 O Sacred Head, Now Wounded

Responsive Liturgy #286 If We Had Been There

Pastoral Prayer

Solo #265 I Know a Fount

Scripture Lesson

Offering and Offertory

Doxology

Meditation

Hymn #427 I Lay My Sins on Jesus

Self-Examination Readings from Psalm 139

The Service of Holy Communion

Hymn #358 Christ, We Do All Adore Thee

Benediction

Postlude #278 There is a Green Hill Far Away

Wedding Service Ideas

The Prelude

Seating of the Mothers

Solo

The Lighting of Candles
(Enter Minister, Best Man, Groomsmen, and Bridegroom)

Introduction to the Ceremony

Minister　On behalf of . . . . and . . . . , I invite you to share in this act of worship in which they will become one, as husband and wife, as intimate friends, as the founders of a home, and as potential parents.

The Processional
(Enter the Bridesmaids, Father of the Bride and the Bride.)

A Hymn of Worship #525 Now Thank We All Our God

Minister　Our main purpose in being here today is to honor God, for it is He who has so guided and shaped the destiny of . . . . and . . . . to make them right and suitable for each other.

Without His leading they would never have met;

Without His grace they would be incapable of loving each other as they do;

And only with His help will they be able to give to the other the inspiration, strength, and stability that will make their's a rich, vital, and growing relationship, one which not only gives them satisfaction but brings gladness to the heart of God.

For all this we praise God, sharing their joy and praying with them that their life together may be rich and full and holy.

A Prayer

A Solo

Minister　At the beginning of the Bible, we discover the first instance of the marriage state when Adam discovers Eve and exlaims, "This at last is bone from my bones and flesh from my flesh." So intimate is this oneness between male and female that in the New Testament St. Paul uses it to illustrate the closeness between Christ and the Church. He further advises that each man should have his own wife, and each woman her own husband. He also draws a clear line separating the distinctive functions of husband and wife, when he instructs the woman to be subject to her husband as to the Lord, and orders the man to love his wife as Christ has loved the church, giving himself up for her.

Minister (addressing Bride and Groom)

. . . . and . . . . marriage is established by God. In this contract a man and woman willingly bind themselves together in love and become one, even as Christ is one with the Church, His Body.

Who gives this woman to this man?

Father of the Bride
I do (or "her mother and I do.")

Scripture Reading #683 I Corinthians 13:1-13

Hymn #530 O Perfect Love

Minister Before you make your individual vows, I would like to solicit from you some promises which have to do with your relationship to God, for only as you rest in Him as the source of power and strength will you be able to bring to each other the vitality that will make yours a living, growing union.

Do you pledge, now in God's presence and in front of your families and friends:

To love God first in your affections,

To think as God thinks by the serious study of Scripture,

To respond to the workings of the Holy Spirit in your individual hearts,

To confess all known sin to God and to be honest in admitting those failings in which you injure each other,

To keep the vows you are now making when they are hardest to fulfill,

To maintain fellowship with other Christians,

To support and pray for each other with compassion and humor and affection?

Bride and Groom (Together)
With God's help, we do.

Minister . . . . & . . . . , God, in His goodness, has brought
you to this solemn moment in which you are to commit
yourselves to each other. While your loved ones take note of
your words and as you stand together in the presence of God,
make your vows the one to the other.

Minister   (addressing the Bridegroom)

. . . . . . , do you take . . . . as your wife? Do you give
her your solemn word, as a sign of your faith in her and love for
her? Do you respect her for her strengths and love her for her
weaknesses? Do you appreciate her for the unique person she
is, a person fashioned and prepared for you in the providence of
God?

Do you promise to support her; to undertake full responsibility for her; to shelter and protect her? Do you trust her? Will you
stay with her, never leaving her, and make a home with her after
the pattern for Christian marriage commanded by God and
described in the Scripture?

Groom

I do, and I will.

Minister (addressing the Bride)

. . . . , do you take . . . . as your husband? Do
you give him your solemn word, as a sign of your faith in him
and love for him? Do you promise to submit to him in obedience
as the Bible teaches? Do you respect him for his strengths and
love him for his weaknesses? Do you appreciate him for the
unique person he is, a person fashioned by God and prepared
for you in the providence of God?

Do you promise to care for Him? Will you treat him with
consideration? Will you stay with him, never leaving him, and
make a home with him after the pattern for Christian marriage
commanded by God and described in the Scriptures?

Bride

I do, and I will.

Groom (taking the Bride's hand)

I, ... , take you, ... ,to be my wife, and I promise,
with God's help, to be your faithful husband, to love and to care for
you as Christ commands me to do, as long as we live.

Bride (taking the Groom's hand)

I, ... , take you, ... , to be my husband, and I
promise, with God's help, to be your faithful wife, and to love and to
care for you as Christ commands me to do, as long as we live.

The Presentation of the Rings

Groom (placing the ring on the Bride's finger)
Wear this ring as a constant reminder of my love for you.

Bride (placing the ring on the Groom's finger)
Wear this ring as a constant reminder of my love for you.

Prayer (Bride and Groom kneeling)
Father, we have joined this man and woman with all the means at our disposal, but we know our frailty and so we ask You to add Your unseen grace to what we do, that Your spirit may strengthen them in the inner man and hold them together when all else strives to pull them apart. May grace, mercy and peace, from God the Father, God the Son, and God, the Holy Spirit, rest upon you now and evermore. Amen.

The Candle Ceremony

Hymn #440 The Lord's Prayer

Sermon (optional)

Scripture Lesson Ephesians 5:21-28, 33.

Closing Prayer
Eternal God, without whose grace no promise is sure, strengthen . . . . and . . . . with the gift of the Holy Spirit, that they may live out the vows made before You here today. Fill them with Your love and Your joy that they may build a strong and enduring marriage and home. Guide them through Your word to serve You all their life together. Through Jesus Christ, our Lord, to whom be honor and glory for ever and ever, Amen.

Benediction

Presentation of Bride and Groom

Recessional

The Candle Ceremony
The Candle Ceremony in its simplest form requires three candles. The two outer candles are lighted, one by the groom, one by the bride, symbolizing the separate life they have been leading together. They take a taper, lighting the middle candle, symbolizing their oneness as a married couple. With a snuffer, they then extinguish the two outer candles as they hold the snuffer together. The arrangement of the candles and the placement of them is a matter for the bride to decide.

Solos
It is advisable for the pastor or minister of music to insist on the right to

supervise all music used by soloists. It may be best to ask the singer to suggest a number of possibilities, thus ensuring that the music used is familiar to the soloist, but granting the church the right to veto a song that is deemed inappropriate to a Christian ceremony. It can be pointed out to the couple, during pre-marital counselling, that the church reserves the right to insist that all parts of the wedding be honoring to Christ. In view of the fact that some singers may not know anything in the devotional repertoire, a book such as *Whom God Hath Joined Together* may be helpful. (B-G0670, Fred Bock Music Co) This volume also contains some contemporary wedding music as well as a number of solo pieces.

Hymns

Congregational hymns are coming back into fashion at weddings. Where the ceremony is well attended and the majority of the guests are familiar with hymn singing, their use is a wonderful way of giving opportunity for the congregation to participate in the occasion. A wedding, like any other event in church, is a service of worship. God is the key figure, not the bride and groom. Thus a hymn of worship and thanksgiving creates the proper reverent atmosphere desirable for a ceremony in which the couple shares a deep personal faith in Christ.

The following hymns, in addition to those listed in this order of service, are suitable for a wedding:

#21 Love Divine, All Love's Excelling
#535 In the Circle of Each Home
#605 If You Will Only Let God Guide You
#601 Savior, Like a Shepherd Lead Us
#323 Holy, Holy, Holy! Lord God Almighty
#66 My Shepherd Will Supply My Need
#40 & 42 The Lord's My Shepherd
(See also Topical Index "Marriage")

Scripture Readings
(suitable for use in the marriage ceremony)

#41 Psalm 23
#388 His Love Is Everlasting
#683 I Corinthians 13:1-13
#529 Marriage
#531 Womanhood (Proverbs 31:10-21, 23, 25-30)
#532 Manhood

A Service of Baptism or Dedication of Children

Welcome and Announcements

Prelude Improvisation on Hymn #15, Jesus Loves the Little Children

The Call to Worship

Opening Hymn #547 The Church's One Foundation

Reading (unison) #558 The People of God

Prayer

Choir Anthem #543 The Family of God

Scripture Reading

Solo #265 I Know a Fount

Reading #561 Thanksgiving

Offering and Offertory

Doxology #382

Sermon Scripture

The Sermon "The Meaning of Baptism"

Reading #569 Welcoming a Child

Hymn #571 This Child We Dedicate to Thee

The Service of Baptism

Hymn #535 In the Circle of Each Home

Benediction

Postlude

A Service of Adult Baptism

(An Evening Service)

Prelude

Choral Introit #621 Turn Your Eyes Upon Jesus

Prayer

Welcome

Hymn Sing: #618 I Will Sing the Wondrous Story
#581 It Is No Secret

Reading #583 God's Power in our Weakness

Choir Anthem #575 If My People Will Pray

Scripture Reading

Informal Prayer from Congregation

Offering and Offertory

Hymn #461 Jesus, We Just Want to Thank You

Sermon "The Meaning of Baptism"

Hymn #276 Come to Calvary's Holy Mountain

The Service of Baptism
(Hymns may be sung by the congregation during the rite of baptism,
or by the choir.)
#266 Nothing But the Blood
#298 Christ Arose
#263 There Is a Fountain Filled With Blood
#262 The Blood Will Never Lose Its Power
#258 When I Survey the Wondrous Cross
#259 Are You Washed in the Blood?
#244 Jesus! What a Friend for Sinners

Benediction

Postlude

Funeral or Memorial Service Ideas

Prelude #48 There Is a Balm in Gilead

Call to Worship

Hymn #51 I Heard the Voice of Jesus Say

Call to Praise
   Leader: The Lord is risen.
   People: The Lord is risen indeed.
   Leader: We worship Him who once proclaimed.
           "I am the resurrection and the life:
           He who believes in me, though he die
           yet shall he live, and whoever lives
           and believes in me shall never die."
   People: We praise you, Lord, that death is defeated.
   Leader: We praise you, Lord, that one of your sons (daughters) is now
           more alive than he (she) has ever been.
   People: Yet we are saddened, Lord, our grief is great.
   Leader: The Lord gave and the Lord has taken away.
   People: Blessed be the name of the Lord.
   Leader: What is the nature of our grief?
   People: Death has come to us. We have lost our loved one.
           We recognize that we shall be lonely.
           Death has come. It is for this that we grieve.
           But we are not as those who grieve without hope.
           For for we are certain that death, far from being the end,
           is the beginning of better things for God's people.
           But still we must express our sorrow.
   Leader: God understands these feelings, this grief.
           He speaks to us now through a song of David
           using his words for our comfort.
   People: #41 Psalm 23

Hymn #37 The Hiding Place

Reading #50 God Is For Us

Solo/Choir #43 Through It All

Eulogy and/or Tributes by family and friends

The Sermon

Hymn #98 Great Is Thy Faithfulness

Readings by Minister (excerpts from the following may be used.)

> I Corinthians 15
> Romans 8
> II Corinthians 4
> I Thessalonians 4
> Revelation 7
> John 14

Prayer

> Loving Heavenly Father,
>> We sorrow, but in hope.
>> We grieve, but in peace.
>> We question, but we trust you
>>> and resolve to let you be God in this
>>> as in all of life's situations.
>> We feel impoverished by the absence of . . . .
>>> because his (her) life so enriched us,
>>> and the degree of our loss is proof
>>> of how much you gave to us through this unique human being.
> Father, meet us in our heartbreak and shock at the finality of death
>> and help us to open up our hearts
>> to receive all the comfort you wish to give us. Amen.

Call to Praise

> Leader: The Lord has given.
> The Lord has taken that which He loaned to us.
> People: Christ went before us in death. Our friend and loved one has gone before us in death. Both are showing us the way into eternal life.
> Leader: We're thankful for all that God gave us of Himself through
> . . . .
> People: We're glad that he (she) is now in the very presence of the Lord.
> Leader: We no longer fear death now that we see it as the way to God.
> People: We know that we shall all die. But we believe that death is not the end. Death is the means by which we pass from flesh and blood into the Spiritual Kingdom.

Hymn #292 Because He Lives

Benediction

Postlude

(In most instances the Funeral proper will be separate from the Graveside service).

cAdditional Topical/Theme Ideas

A Service of Worship

Worship Theme: The Good Shepherd (John 10:1-8)

Prelude #66 My Shepherd Will Supply My Need

Choral Introit #61 Like a Lamb Who Needs the Shepherd

Call to Worship
   Leader: I give you a great statement from the lips of Christ.
          Think it through.
          He said, "I AM THE GOOD SHEPHERD."
          Those few words reveal something of the care and love
            which Christ brings to you now.
   People: As those who have gone astray,
          we come back into the fold.
          As those who are stained and sullied,
          we ask to be washed clean.
          As those who are hungry,
          we seek to be fed.
          As those who wander aimlessly,
            we desire to be led by the Spirit into all Truth.
          As those who are hurt and wounded,
            we ask for healing of mind, spirit and body. Amen.

Hymn #42 The Lord's My Shepherd, I'll Not Want

Unison Reading #41 Psalm 23

Prayer of Confession

Assurance of Forgiveness
   Leader: How wonderful it is, Lord, to be forgiven.
   People: How great it is to be accepted as we are.
   Leader: It encourages us to know that You never give up on us, for You
          continue Your good work in us until we come to resemble
          Jesus Christ.
   People: Our Father in Heaven; your name is holy. May your kingdom
          come, may your will be done on earth as it is in Heaven. Give
          us today the food we need. Forgive us for what we owe to

You, as we have also forgiven those who owe us anything. Keep us clear of temptation, and save us from evil. For the Kingdom, the Power and the Glory are yours. Amen.

Anthem #53 Cast Thy Burden Upon the Lord.

Reading #90 Hope

Pastoral Prayer

Announcements

Offertory Sentence

Offering and Offertory

Hymn #94 I Am Not Skilled to Understand

The Sermon

Hymn #601 Savior, Like a Shepherd Lead Us

Benediction

Postlude #600 Take Thou My Hand, O Father

A Service of Worship

Worship Theme: Guidance (James 1:5-8)

Prelude #40 The Lord's My Shepherd, I'll Not Want

Call to Worship
  Leader: Delight in the Lord. Then He will give you all your heart's desire.
  People: Commit everything you do to Him, trust Him to help you do it, and He will.
  Leader: Rest in the Lord. Relax in the quiet trust that He cares for you.
  People: Wait patiently for Him to act. Don't envy godless people who seem to prosper more than you do.
  Leader: All who humble themselves before the Lord shall be given great rewards and even now have the peace that passes understanding.
  People: If we err, it isn't fatal, for we have found an antidote for sin. The weaknesses that used to drive us from God, now turn us to Him.
  WE ARE A FORGIVEN PEOPLE, PRAISE BE TO GOD. AMEN.

Hymn #606 He Leadeth Me, O Blessed Thought

Reading #599 Freedom of the Will

Prayer

Anthem #595 Lead on, O King Eternal

Announcements

Offering and Offertory

Prayer (Unison)
>   Father, for the satisfaction and rewards of our work;
>   for the strength and sanity to function;
>   for the freedom to choose our life's vocation;
>   for the sense of achievement and accomplishment that is ours
>   from work well done;
>   for all these blessings we give thanks, expressing our apprecia-
>   tion in this act of worship and in the money we now present to
>   you. Amen.

Hymn #597 God Leads Us Along

Scripture Lesson

The Sermon

Closing Hymn #605 If You Will Only Let God Guide You

Benediction

Choral Postlude #596 Gentle Shepherd

A Service of Worship

Theme: God, the Creator (Genesis 1, 2 & John 1:1-5)

Prelude #4 God, Who Made the Earth and Heaven

Choral Introit #5 Morning Has Broken
>   Leader: The heavens declare the glory of God.
>   People: The vault of heaven reveals His handiwork.
>   Leader: Day speaks of it to day.
>   People: Night to night passes on the knowledge.
>   Leader: What have you seen today that reminds you of God's artistry
>   and creativity?
>   People: He has made another morning.
>   We have seen the sky and the earth.
>   Last night we saw the stars.
>   At dawn we witnessed in the West the birth of a new day.

Leader: O, God, I gaze into the heavens,
created by You, maintained by You,
and I ask myself, "What is the human race that You lavish so
much love upon it?"

People: And what am I that, out of all the billions of people on the face
of the globe, You know me and love me in a personal way?

Unison: We praise You, Lord, that You have made us a little less than
God, that You have made us capable of containing your deity,
that You have put yourself inside us in the Holy Spirit. All this
is too wonderful, too wonderful. What can we say except,
THANKS BE TO GOD FOR HIS UNSPEAKABLE GIFT.

Hymn of Praise #6 This Is My Father's World

Prayer

Solo #13 The Wonder of It All

Reading #11 Psalm 104

Pastoral Prayer

Lord's Prayer #440 (Sung in unison)

Announcements

Offering and Offertory

Doxology

Hymn #10 Earth and All Stars

Anthem #20 God So Loved the World

The Sermon

Closing Hymn #2 How Great Thou Art

Benediction

Postlude #381 All People That on Earth Do Dwell

A Service of Worship

Theme: Christ, the Head of the Church (Ephesians 1:15-23)

Prelude

Welcome and Announcements

Choral Introit #321 Brethren, We Have Met to Worship

Call to Worship
  Leader: In the beginning was the Word.
  People: And the Word was with God,
          And the Word was God.
  Leader: He was in the beginning with God.
          Through Him all things came to be.
  People: Not one thing had its being but through Him.
  Leader: All that came to be had life in Him.
          And that life was the light of men,
            A light that shines in the dark,
            A light that darkness cannot overpower.
  Unison: Lighten our darkness, we beseech Thee, O Lord. Amen.

Hymn #557 Christ Is Made the Sure Foundation

Prayer

Unison Reading #558 The People of God

Anthem #575 If My People Will Pray

Pastoral Prayer

Sermon Scripture

The Sermon

Hymn #547 The Church's One Foundation

Offering and Offertory

Dedication of the Offering (Unison)
  Father, with these gifts, we make a renewal of our pledge to love You
  with all our hearts and to serve You with all our enthusiasm. We
  express to You our resolve to worship You alone, and our determina-
  tion to work hard to build Your church in today's world. Amen.

Hymn #440 The Lord's Prayer (sung in unison)

The Blessing
  God has been with us in our gathering. He will be with us as we scatter
  and go our separate ways. Remember that He has promised never to
  leave us, never to forsake us, but to be with us always. Be blessed by
  this reminder. Amen.

Postlude #560 Blest Be the Tie That Binds.

A Service of Worship

Theme: Unity in the Church—The Family of God (I Corinthians 12:4, 14:1a)

Prelude #476 More Love to Thee, O Christ

Call to Worship
Leader: We are gathered for worship, as members of a spiritual family, as cells in the Body.
People: Our expectations are high, for we are not like any other society of people. We are God's people, and we are together in obedience to a divine commandment.
Leader: Let's be happy together, celebrating our oneness, for we are here
In the name of the Father who made us originally,
In the name of the Son who makes us free,
In the name of the Spirit who makes us one.

Hymn #546 We Are God's People

Prayer #549 Prayer for Unity

Unison Reading #553 Psalm 15

Solo #548 Getting Used to the Family of God

Pastoral Prayer

Scripture Reading

A time of informal sharing and prayer

Hymn #556 There's a Quiet Understanding

Offering and Offertory

Doxology

Reading #561 Thanksgiving

Hymn #551 There's a Church Within Us, O Lord

The Sermon

Hymn #677 They'll Know We Are Christians by Our Love

The Blessing (in unison)
May the grace of Christ which daily renews us;
And the love of God which enables us to love all men;
And the fellowship of the Holy Spirit which unites us in one body,

keep us keen to discern and prompt to obey
the complete will of God
   until we meet again,
      through Jesus Christ our Lord. Amen.

Postlude

A Service of Worship

Theme: Supremacy of Christ (Isaiah 9:6,7)

Prelude #465 Jesus, the Very Thought of Thee

Hymn #468 Be Thou My Vision

Call to Worship
   Leader: What is the chief end of man?
   People: Our chief end is to glorify God and to enjoy Him forever.
   Leader: All of life must be a celebration of our relationship with Him.
   People: This is the continuing wonder of it, that a God so pure and
           unflawed eagerly welcomes into His presence pardoned sin-
           ners.
   Leader: Let's remind ourselves of the warmth of God's invitation in
           the words of our opening hymn.

Hymn #276 Come to Calvary's Holy Mountain

Meditation *(read by Worship Leader)*
   "Who are you, really? Who, if not the Lord God?
   You are the acme, the pinnacle of everything; of goodness, power,
   mercy, justice, beauty, strength; of hiddenness and nearness; of
   stability and mystery. You are unchanging and yet you change
   everything. You are new, never old; yet you make all things new. You
   humiliate the proud without their knowing it. You are always active,
   always resting; gathering yet needing nothing; bearing, fulfilling,
   protecting, creating, nourishing, perfecting, seeking what you don't
   need. You love without getting involved with passion. You are
   jealous, yet you remain unconcerned. You repent, but without being
   sorry. You become angry, yet you stay serene. You change your
   operations, but never your plans. You recover what you did not lose in
   the first place. Never in want, you rejoice at what you have won. Never

greedy, you exact regular interest. . . . But what have I really been saying, God my life, my delight? What can anyone say about you?"[1]

Reading (Unison) #233 The Supremacy of Christ

Hymn #232 Join All the Glorious Names

Pastoral Prayer (concluding with The Lord's Prayer)

Choir Anthem #238 Jesus Shall Reign Where'er the Sun

Scripture for Sermon

The Sermon

Hymn #230 His Name Is Wonderful

Offering and Offertory

Doxology

Benediction

Choir Response #699 Sixfold Amen

A Service of Worship

Theme: Renewal in the Church (Isaiah 5:5, Revelation 3:15)

Meditation #577 Comparison

Prelude

Call to Worship
  Leader: Do you not know? Have you not heard? The everlasting God, the Lord, the creator of the ends of the earth does not become weary or tired. His understanding is inscrutable.
  People: He gives strength to the weary, and to him who lacks might He increases power.
  Leader: Though youths grow weary and tired, and vigorous young men stumble badly,
  People: Yet those who wait for the Lord will gain new strength; they will mount up with wings like eagles;

[1]Sherwood Wirt. Love Song—*a new translation of Augustine's Confessions.* New York: Harper & Row, 1971.

they will run and not get tired;
they will walk and not become weary. (Isaiah 40)

Hymn #576 Thou, Whose Purpose is to Kindle

Reading #578 II Chronicles 7:8-18

Prayer

Anthem #575 If My People Will Pray

Scripture Lesson

Solo #579 O Breath of Life

Announcements

Offering and Offertory

Doxology

Hymn #580 There Shall Be Showers of Blessing

The Sermon

Hymn #572 Renew Thy Church, Her Ministries Restore

Prayer

Benediction

Postlude

A Service of Worship

Theme: Mission to the World (II Corinthians 5:17)

Meditation #673 Precious in God's Sight

Prelude #648 I'll Tell the World That I'm a Christian

Call to Worship (Unison) #643 Christ Be With Me

Hymn #669 Hear the Voice of Jesus Calling

Prayer

Solo #655 Reach Out and Touch

Reading #666 Vision (Revelation 7:9-17)

Hymn #662 Let Your Heart Be Broken

Announcements

Offering and Offertory

Doxology

Pastoral Prayer

Testimony from Missionary or Missionary Candidate

Anthem #658 O, Zion, Haste, Thy Mission High Fulfilling

Scripture Reading

Hymn #664 So Send I You

The Sermon

Hymn #672 Through All the World

Anthem #652 Get All Excited

Benediction

Postlude

A Service of Worship

Theme: Comfort in Affliction (Hebrews 12:3-17)

Meditation #111 A Certain Uncertain Future

Prelude #590 I Am His and He Is Mine

Call to Worship #17 Psalm 89 (in unison)

Hymn #608 Guide Me, O Thou Great Jehovah

Reading #593 Take His Peace

Prayer

Anthem #601 Savior, Like a Shepherd Lead Us

Reading #583 God's Power in Our Weaknesses

Pastoral Prayer

Solo #584 God Is at Work Within You

Announcements

Offering and Offertory

Doxology

Scripture Lesson #490 Psalm 83 (in unison)

Anthems #493 Thou Wilt Keep Him in Perfect Peace

Hymn #603 God Moves in a Mysterious Way

The Sermon

Hymn #112 He Giveth More Grace

The Blessing (in unison)
O, Lord, support us all the day long of this troubled life, until the shades lengthen, and the evening comes, and the busy world is hushed, and the fever of life is over and our work is done. Then, Lord, in your mercy grant us a safe lodging, a holy rest, and peace at the last. Through Jesus Christ, our Lord. Amen.

Hymn #149 Holy, Holy

Postlude #91 'Tis So Sweet to Trust in Jesus.

Four Standard Worship Services

I
A Service of Worship

Prelude #102 Day By Day and With Each Passing Moment

Welcome and Announcements

Call to Worship (in Unison)
    The Lord is in His holy temple.
    Let all the earth keep silent before Him.
    Surely the Lord is in this place.
    This is none other than the house of God,
        and this is the gate of Heaven.
    God is a Spirit and they who worship Him
        must worship Him in Spirit and in truth.

Hymn #323 Holy! Holy! Holy! Lord God Almighty

The Te Deum #324 (in unison)

Anthem #339 Praise My Soul, The King of Heaven

Prayer #355 We Thank You, Father

Scripture Readings
    Old Testament
    New Testament

Pastoral Prayer

Hymn #365 My Tribute

The Offering and Offertory

The Doxology

Prayer

The Sermon

Hymn #474 Eternal Life

Prayer #506 Make Us Worthy, Lord

Benediction

Postlude #507 Come, All Christians, Be Committed

II
A Service of Worship

*Prelude**

Call to Worship #340 A Call to Worship

Hymn #338 We Sing the Greatness of Our God

Worship #329 Worship

Prayer

Reading #375 Praises to the Lord

Anthem Let God Be God*

Scripture Lesson

Pastoral Prayer

Solo #102 Day by Day and With Each Passing Moment

Offering and Offertory

Doxology

Prayer (in unison)

Lord, it is in our power to use or to abuse every gift you have given us. These alternatives concern us now. Help us to make the right choices; to hold our resources in trust rather than to squander them in selfish indulgence; to think of serving others before we think of being catered to ourselves. Make us eager to love one another, and help us to pool our talents and strengths for the good of the body of Christ.

We bring these gifts to you in the name of Him who, though he was rich, for our sakes became poor that we, through His poverty, might be made exceeding rich. Amen.

The Sermon

Hymn #81 Let God Be God

Announcements

The Blessing (Unison)

The Spirit of Christ go with you into the coming week.

Postlude #140 Hymn to the Trinity

---

*The anthem, in this instance, familiarizes the congregation with the hymn, which is then used later in the service. It could be introduced by the organist using it as a prelude, so that the congregation becomes familiar with the melody.

III
A Service of Worship

Prelude Improvisation on Hymn #5 Morning Has Broken

(See Organ Selections Based on Hymns found in
Hymns for the Family of God, page 135.)

A Time of Praise

Hymn #339 Praise My Soul, The King of Heaven

Reading #375 Praises to the Lord

Hymn #319 Immortal, Invisible, God Only Wise

Reading (in unison) #119 A Contemporary Te Deum

A Time of Confession

Reading #418 The General Confession

Hymn #417 Just As I Am, Without One Plea

Responsive Reading #50 God Is For Us

Pastoral Prayer (concluding with The Lord's Prayer)

A Time of Sharing

The Sermon Lesson

Hymn #544 The Bond of Love

Shared Concerns and Prayers

Announcements

Offering and Offertory

The Doxology

A Time of Instruction

The Sermon

Prayer #383 Prayer

Hymn #505 Your Cause Be Mine

The Spoken Blessing

Choral Benediction #522 The Lord Bless You and Keep You

Postlude

IV
A Service of Worship

Prelude

Welcome and Announcements

Call to Worship
    Leader: Lift up your hearts
    People: We lift them up to the Lord.
    Leader: Let us be thankful in His presence.
    People: It is appropriate that we should give thanks for the Lord's continuing protection and provision.
    Leader: It is our duty at all times to appreciate the blessings of God, even in a time of sorrow, for He is our comfort, and in a time of trial, for He is our escape.
    People: Great is the Lord, and greatly to be praised. All other gods are unreal. He alone is authentic deity. He alone deserves our love, our time, our sacrifice and our service.
    All: We praise You, our Father, that You have revealed to us Your Light and have shown us Your Way. There is no one with whom to compare You; You are unique, without rival, God of Gods and King of Kings. Amen.

Hymn #321 Brethren, We Have Met to Worship

Invocation

The Lord's Prayer

Scripture Reading

A Prayer for Comfort #88 When We Feel Forsaken

A Hymn of Comfort #89 Children of the Heavenly Father

The Pastoral Prayer

The Ministry of Music

Offering and Offertory

Prayer #506 Make Us Worthy, Lord

The Sermon

Hymn #551 There's a Church Within Us, O Lord

Benediction Prayer (in unison)
　All through this week, O Lord, let me touch the lives of others for good, by the power of your quickening Spirit, whether through the words I speak, the prayers I breathe, or the life I live. In the name of Jesus, Amen.

IV

Expanded Use of the Hymnal

A Hymnal at Home Is a Wonderful Thing

By Gloria Gaither

Most families would like to worship together at home, but many are embarrassed to start; some do not know where to begin to assemble materials—books, pictures, etc. Some have wished for help in planning for worship while away from home on vacations, or family outings.

Hymns for the Family of God is the perfect place to begin, because it is adaptable to almost any situation and has materials that speak to all ages.

Here are a few suggestions you should keep in mind for your worship times:

- While it is sometimes good to have a set time for worship, be ready to take advantage of the most teachable moments. Some particular experience may make it better to have worship at another time—after a game of tennis, a good swim, a picnic, and even after a sad experience, worship may be far more meaningful.
- Without being rigid, try to keep the worship time short. If there are weighty problems, needs or concerns which require long, earnest prayer, do not consider it at family worship except perhaps briefly.
- Be sure to give the whole family a chance to contribute. Even small children often have great insight.
- Use whatever talent each person has: reading, singing, playing musical instruments such as a guitar, autoharp, piano, praying, speaking.
- Encourage the less gifted child to participate without interruption.
- While reverence and order are important, this is not a formal church service; make it flexible. Keep it happy with room for the Holy Spirit to add or subtract from your material and preparation.
- Begin where the children are, but do not underestimate the ability of a child to understand spiritual things and to learn quickly.

There is a wealth of songs in *Hymns for the Family of God* that have already become favorites with contemporary young people. Most have simple words and harmony that could well become standards in your family circle. Encourage your youngsters to learn to play these on their instruments as well as sing them.

#361 Alleluia
#560 Blest Be the Tie That Binds
#543 The Family of God
#414 Father, I Adore You (sung as a round)
#652 Get All Excited (use guitar, drums, autoharp, etc.)
#234 He Is Lord
#632 He's Everything to Me
#628 He Touched Me (chorus)
#230 His Name Is Wonderful
#648 I'll Tell the World That I'm a Christian
#581 It Is No Secret
#226 Jesus Loves Me, This I Know
  #15 Jesus Loves the Little Children
#461 Jesus, We Just Want to Thank You
#421 Lord I Want To Be a Christian
#367 Lord, We Praise You
  #5 Morning Has Broken
#365 My Tribute
#622 O, How He Loves You and Me
#641 Pass It On
#655 Reach Out and Touch
#656 Something Beautiful
  #13 The Wonder of It All
#677 They'll Know We Are Christians By Our Love
#693 This Is My Country
#544 We Are One in the Bond of Love

This list is not meant to limit you; it is meant only to give your family a place to begin. Don't be afraid to use the stately old hymns and time-proven gospel songs. These songs may not be new, but your children are a new generation. Let the freshness of your children's keen insights inspire *you* once again.

In your own family you will find lots of creative ideas for using the resources in this book. Older children are great planners, too, and your trust in giving them the responsibility of an occasional family worship time is good for their Christian growth. But just to help you, here are a few specific suggestions:

Being God's Person Today
    Read: #675 Prayer of Concern for Others

Read: Romans 12: 9-18 (Living Bible)
Sing: #677 They'll Know We Are Christians By Our Love

Forgiveness and Joy ✓
Sing: #414 Father, I Adore You (as a round)
Read: #413 The Good News of God's Forgiveness (divide family in two groups)
Sing: #317 Let's Just Praise the Lord

Patriotic Day (public election, July 4th, when one child is involved in study of government, when international issue is dominating news.)
Sing: #693 This Is My Country
Read: lyrics to #682 A Song of Peace, and discuss
Read: #683 I Corinthians 13: 1-13. Discuss passage in relation to national affairs and our attitudes as Christians
Sing: #677 They'll Know We Are Christians By Our Love, or play a recording of #575 If My People Will Pray

When Teen-ager Is Going Through Time of Doubt or Confusion ✓
Read: #604 The Tangle of the Mind
Read: #602 James 1: 5-8
Sing: #656 Something Beautiful or use reading of #583 God's Power In Our Weakness with the song #596 Gentle Shepherd

When Death, Disappointment, Divorce or Tragedy Has Touched a Friend or Member of the Family ✓
Read: #542 Prayer (Parent)
Share: Talk about the hurt in the world and how we can be Jesus to those who need mending.
Sing: #655 Reach Out and Touch, or
         #677 They'll Know We Are Christians By Our Love, or use one of the comforting hymns:
         #49 I Must Tell Jesus
         #443 I Need Thee

Celebrating God's Gift of Children (birthday, special award, honor) ✓
Read: #211 Jesus and the Children
Sing: #226 Jesus Loves Me, This I Know, or
         #225 Jesus Loves Even Me

Share: Have family members tell what is special to them about each
person.

Affirming Our Beliefs

Create: A series of worship times using various statements of faith:
#137 The Apostles' Creed
#138 The Nicene Creed
#139 An Affirmation
#141 We Believe In A Triune God.

Songs that could be used include:
#75 My Faith Has Found a Resting Place
#92 The Solid Rock
#96 I Know Who Holds Tomorrow
#67 Blessed Assurance
#84 My Faith Looks Up To Thee
#82 Victory In Jesus

Write: (for the last session) A statement of your own called "The
(*Your last name*)Believe." Let the children contribute in their
own words what you have come to believe and why.

Celebration for the Family

Read: #14 A Celebration for Family People. One person reads
while others answer.

To Begin a New Day

Read: #643 Christ Be with Me
Sing: #5 Morning Has Broken. Use flute or trumpet if someone
plays it.
Read: Psalm 5: 1-3

When Someone Is Discouraged

Read: #615 The Temptation to Quit
Sing: #621 Turn Your Eyes Upon Jesus
Read: Romans 8: 31-39 (Living Bible or Phillips)

When a New Baby Comes into the Family Circle

Adapt: #569 Welcoming a Child
Assign parts to various children and read the last prayer
together (using "our family") as a family pledge to the new
child.
Sing: #596 Gentle Shepherd
#367 Lord, We Praise You
#461 Jesus, We Just Want to Thank You

Thanksgiving

Read: #561 Thanksgiving
Substituting "family" for "Church", or
#391 Thanksgiving Day
Sing: #367 Lord, We Praise You or
#461 Jesus, We Just Want to Thank You
Pray: Have each person offer a sentence prayer for something specific in his/her life.

On Growing to Be a Man

Read: #532 Manhood
Sing: #421 Lord, I Want to Be a Christian

For Parents or Parents-to-be

Read: #534 The Parents' Creed. (Read by parent.)
Sing: #540 Happy the Home When God Is There
Pray: That it may be so.

On Family Vacation ✓

Read: #549 Prayer for Unity
Share: Have a listening time; let each person share what he has heard.
Sing: #361 Alleluia
Make up extra stanzas to suit the situation as:
"For the beauty, Lord, we thank Thee . . ." or
"Help us hear you, and be grateful . . ."
Read: Psalm 121
Option: #317 Let's Just Praise the Lord.

Easter

Read: #302 He Is Risen!
#294 Easter
Mark 16: 1-6
Songs: #301 The Easter Song (may use one of many available recordings)
#292 Because He Lives (chorus)
#299 He Lives (chorus)
#234 He Is Lord

Christmas

Use records or sing with piano, bells, triangles, trumpet, flute, autoharp, or anything else available, for dozens of combinations to create meaningful worship times during the whole Christmas season. Use especially the Scripture John 1:1-14, #165 Beginning.

Solo, Duet, Trio, and Quartet Selections
BASED ON HYMNS FOUND IN
"HYMNS FOR THE FAMILY OF GOD"

By Douglas Lawrence

This listing of solo, duet, trio and quartet possibilities from "Hymns for the Family of God" is meant to spark your creativity. Almost any hymn found in this book could easily be used as a solo, or in some other voice combination. The listing which follows simply indicates some of the more obvious choices. The following performance notes might also be helpful to you as you make your selections, and as you sing:

1. Any piece listed as a solo could most likely be sung also as a duet, borrowing from the three other parts for harmony.
2. Anything listed as a trio is meant to be used with soprano, alto, and tenor parts. There may be times when a note will need to be borrowed from the bass line in order to complete the necessary harmonic structure.
3. All of the selections work well as quartets. The harmonizations found in *Hymns for the Family of God* are excellent for this purpose. Most of them would work well as male quartets if you have the bass read the regular bass line; the baritone read the alto line; second tenor read the melody line; and first tenor read the regular tenor line.

Amazing Grace	107	Solo
America, the Beautiful	690	Solo
At the Name of Jesus	351	Solo/Guitar
Battle Hymn of the Republic	692	Solo
Because He Lives	292	Solo
Blessed Jesus	39	Solo/Trio
Blessed Quietness	145	Trio
Burdens Are Lifted at Calvary	60	Solo/Trio/Quartet
Child in the Manger	198	Solo
Children of the Heavenly Father	89	Trio/Quartet
Cleanse Me	425	Trio/Quartet

Come, Holy Spirit	150	Trio
Day By Day	102	Quartet
Fill Me Now	153	Trio
Fill My Cup, Lord	481	Trio
Gentle Shepherd	596	Solo
Go, Tell It On the Mountains	205	Solo
God So Loved the World	20	Solo
He Giveth More Grace	112	Solo/Trio
He Touched Me	628	Solo/Trio
He's Everything to Me	632	Solo
He's Still the King of Kings	242	Trio
He's the Savior of My Soul	247	Trio
Holy Spirit, Flow Through Me	164	Quartet
How Great Thou Art	2	Solo/Trio
I Am His and He Is Mine	590	Trio
I Believe in a Hill Called Mount Calvary	270	Trio/Quartet
I Could Never Outlove the Lord	452	Trio
I Know Who Holds Tomorrow	96	Trio
I Wonder As I Wander	183	Solo
I'd Rather Have Jesus	650	Solo
If My People Will Pray	575	Solo
If That Isn't Love	224	Trio
Jesus Walked This Lonesome Valley	217	Trio
Like a Lamb Who Needs the Shepherd	61	Solo/Quartet
Lord, I Want to Be a Christian	421	Solo
Love Was When	28	Solo/Duet
Moment By Moment	65	Trio
Morning Has Broken	5	Solo
My Country, 'Tis Of Thee	695	Solo
My Jesus, I Love Thee	456	Trio
My Lord, What a Morning!	316	Solo
My Shepherd Will Supply My Need	66	Solo
My Tribute	365	Solo
My Wonderful Lord	368	Trio
No One Understands Like Jesus	36	Solo
Now I Belong to Jesus	637	Quartet
O, How He Loves You and Me	622	Solo/Quartet
O Love That Will Not Let Me Go	404	Quartet
Plenty of Room in the Family	552	Trio
Praise Be to Jesus	366	Trio/Quartet
Precious Lord, Take My Hand	611	Solo
Reach Out and Touch	655	Solo

Reach Out to Jesus	430	Trio/Quartet
Redeeming Love	199	Trio
Some Children See Him	181	Solo
Something Worth Living For	638	Trio
Sometimes "Alleluia"	331	Solo/Duet
Sweet, Sweet Spirit	159	Quartet
Thank God for the Promise of Spring	110	Trio
The Blood Will Never Lose Its Power	262	Quartet
The Family of God	543	Solo/Trio
The Hiding Place	37	Solo/Duet
The King Is Coming	313	Solo/Duet/Quartet
The Longer I Serve Him	623	Trio
The Lord's Prayer	440	Solo
The Love of God	18	Solo
The Savior Is Waiting	435	Solo/Quartet
The Spirit of Jesus Is in This Place	157	Duet
The Star Carol	201	Solo
The Star-Spangled Banner	688	Solo
The Wonder of It All	13	Solo/Trio
There's Something About That Name	227	Quartet
They That Sow in Tears	46	Solo
They That Wait Upon the Lord	52	Solo
They'll Know We Are Christians by Our Love	677	Solo
This Could Be the Dawning of That Day	307	Trio
This Is My Country	693	Solo
Through It All	43	Solo/Trio
We Are Climbing Jacob's Ladder	488	Solo
Were You There?	287	Solo
What Wondrous Love Is This?	283	Solo
Where the Spirit of the Lord Is	148	Trio
Worthy the Lamb	285	Quartet
Yesterday, Today and Tomorrow	76	Trio

Children's Choral Selections

BASED ON HYMNS FOUND IN
"HYMNS FOR THE FAMILY OF GOD"

By Lucy A. Hirt

AS A SOURCE of inspiration and information, the hymnal is potentially second only to the Bible, for it exposes children, and adults, too, to theology, good poetry, and history. Prepared to help choral directors with limited time and resources, this listing of materials readily available in *Hymns for the Family of God* will teach hymns, and at the same time, be suitable for performance. Any of the titles suggested will work well as children's choir presentations. There are recommended choral arrangements available where children can participate very easily, (since they will already know the hymntunes) and these have been included under each title in the listing. Many more are available, and new settings are published all the time. It is important for children to have a good groundwork in knowing the standard hymnody of the Church. That they can also perform, alone or in multiple choir situations, is an added benefit of this knowledge of hymns.

Key to symbols:
  ALVH—Alternate last-verse harmonization
  AOrl—Adaptable to Orff-type instrumentation
  D—Descant (vocal, trumpet, handbell)
Page numbers refer to *Hymns for the Family of God.*

TITLE	PAGE	TUNE	PERFORMANCE
A MIGHTY FORTRESS IS OUR GOD	118	*Ein' Feste Burg*	D-vocal
ALL CREATURES OF OUR GOD AND KING	347	*Lasst Uns Erfreuen*	ALVH, AOrl
ALL GLORY, LAUD AND HONOR	249	*St. Theodulph*	ALVH, D-vocal
ALL HAIL THE POWER OF JESUS' NAME	325	*Coronation*	ALVH
ALL PEOPLE THAT ON EARTH DO DWELL arr. Florence Jolley, Lawson-Gould, Inc.,/ G. Schirmer, Inc., 623	381	*Old 100th*	
ALL PRAISE TO THEE, MY GOD arr. Carl Mueller, G. Schirmer, Inc., 11163	518	*Tallis' Canon*	AOrl

TITLE	PAGE	TUNE	PERFORMANCE

ALLELUIA
  SATB, "Praise Hymn", Fred Bock
    Fred Bock Music Company, B-G0306
	361	*Alleluia*	

AMERICA, THE BEAUTIFUL	690	*Materna*	D-vocal
ANGELS FROM THE REALMS OF GLORY	190	*Regent Square*	ALVH

ANGELS WE HAVE HEARD ON HIGH
  arr. Jean Pasquet, Elkan-Vogel/
    Theodore Presser Company.
	192	*Gloria*	AOrl

BATTLE HYMN OF THE REPUBLIC
  arr. Peter Wilhousky, Carl Fischer, Inc., CM-4743
    arr. Roy Ringwald, Shawnee Press, Inc., A-28
	692	*Battle Hymn of*
		    the Republic
			D-vocal,
			  trumpets

BE THOU MY VISION	468	*Slane*	
BREAK FORTH, O BEAUTEOUS HEAVENLY LIGHT	207	*Ermuntre*	
BUILT ON THE ROCK	555	*Kirken*	

CHILD IN THE MANGER
  arr. Fred Bock, Fred Bock Music Company,
    B-G0278
	198	*Bunessan*	AOrl

CHILDREN OF THE HEAVENLY FATHER
  arr. Edwin Liemohn, Schmitt, Hall
    & McCreary, 1723
	89	*Tryggare Kan*
		    Ingen Vara
			AOrl

CHRIST THE LORD IS RISEN TODAY	289	*Easter Hymn*	D-vocal, trumpets
COME, CHRISTIANS, JOIN TO SING	342	*Madrid*	ALVH, Echo choir
COME, THOU ALMIGHTY KING	341	*Italian Hymn*	ALVH
COME, YE THANKFUL PEOPLE, COME	392	*St. George's* *Windsor*	ALVH
CROWN HIM WITH MANY CROWNS	345	*Diademata*	D-vocal

FAIREST LORD JESUS
  arr. Paul Christiansen, "Beautiful Savior",
    Augsburg Publishing House.
	240	*Crusader's Hymn*	

FAITH OF OUR FATHERS	526	*St. Catherine*	D-vocal
FOR THE BEAUTY OF THE EARTH	1	*Dix*	AOrl
GLORIOUS THINGS OF THEE ARE SPOKEN	376	*Austrian Hymn*	ALVH

GOD OF GRACE AND GOD OF GLORY
  alternate text: Guide Me, O Thou Great
    Jehovah, selection #608
	528	*CWM Rhondda*	ALVH, AOrl

GOD OF OUR FATHERS	687	*National Hymn*	LAVH

GOOD CHRISTIAN MEN, REJOICE
  arr. Gustav Holst, "Christmas Day,"
    Galaxy Music Corp. AP34
	177	*In Dulci Jubilo*	AOrl

TITLE	PAGE	TUNE	PERFORMANCE
HARK! THE HERALD ANGELS SING	184	*Mendelssohn*	D-vocal
HOLY, HOLY, HOLY	323	*Nicæa*	AOrl,
			D-vocal
HOSANNA, LOUD HOSANNA	248	*Ellacombe*	AOrl
alternate text:			
We Sing the Greatness of Our God, selection #338			
arr. Fred Bock, "I Sing the Greatness of Our God,"			
Fred Bock Music Company. B-G0120			
I KNOW THAT MY REDEEMER LIVES	295	*Duke Street*	
alternate text: Jesus Shall Reign,			
selection #238			
I WONDER AS I WANDER	183	*I Wonder*	U/ with
			accompaniment
IMMORTAL, INVISIBLE, GOD ONLY WISE	319	*St. Denio*	ALVH
IN CHRIST THERE IS NO EAST OR WEST	685	*St. Peter*	
arr. Clark Gassman, Lexicon Music, Inc. 37534			
JESUS LOVES ME! THIS I KNOW	226	*Jesus Loves Me*	
arr. Fred Bock, "Jesus Knows Me and This			
I Love," Fox Music Publications, B-G0379			
JESUS CHRIST IS RISEN TODAY	297	*Llanfair*	AOrl,
alternate text: "Praise the Lord, His Glories			Echo choir
Show," selection #373			
JESUS, PRICELESS TREASURE	277	*Jesu, Meine Freude*	
JESUS SHALL REIGN WHERE'ER THE SUN	238	*Duke Street*	ALVH
alternate text: "I Know That My Redeemer			
Lives," selection #295			
JOY TO THE WORLD!	171	*Antioch*	AROrl
arr. Fred Bock, "Joy to the World, the Lord			
is Coming," Fred Bock Music Company,			
B-G0180			
JOYFUL, JOYFUL, WE ADORE THEE	377	*Hymn to Joy*	
LEAD ON, O KING ETERNAL	595	*Lancashire*	ALVH,
arr. Van Denman Thompson,			D-vocal
Lorenz Industries, Inc., 9787			
LET ALL THINGS NOW LIVING	389	*Ash Grove*	AOrl,
arr. Katherine K. Davis, E. C. Schirmer, 1770			D-vocal
LO, HOW A ROSE E'ER BLOOMING	174	*Es Ist Ein Ros'*	a cappella
MY COUNTRY, 'TIS OF THEE	695	*America*	D-vocal
MY HOPE IS BUILT	92	*Solid Rock*	ALVH
NOW THANK WE ALL OUR GOD	525	*Nun Danket*	
arr. Heinz Werner Zimmerman, "Psalmkonzert,"			
Concordia Publishing House, 97-4866			

TITLE	PAGE	TUNE	PERFORMANCE
O COME, ALL YE FAITHFUL	193	*Adeste Fideles*	D-vocal
O COME, O COME, EMMANUEL	169	*Veni Emmanuel*	ALVH
O FOR A THOUSAND TONGUES TO SING	349	*Azmon*	D-vocal,
arr. John Ness Beck,			ALVH
Fred Bock Music Company. B-G0308			
O SACRED HEAD, NOW WOUNDED	284	*Passion Chorale*	
O WORSHIP THE KING	336	*Lyons*	ALVH
O ZION, HASTE, THY MISSION HIGH	658	*Tidings*	ALVH
FULFILLING			
PRAISE GOD. FROM WHOM ALL			
BLESSINGS FLOW	382,	*Old 100th*	
arr. Ralph Vaughan Williams,	384		
Oxford University Press, 42.1953			
PRAISE, MY SOUL, THE KING OF HEAVEN	339	*Lauda Anima*	D-handbells
PRAISE THE LORD, HIS GLORIES SHOW	373	*Llanfair*	
alternate text: "Jesus Christ is Risen Today,"			
selection #297			
PRAISE TO THE LORD, THE ALMIGHTY	337	*Lobe Den Herren*	AOrl,
REJOICE, THE LORD IS KING!	374	*Darwall's 148th*	D-handbells
REJOICE, YE PURE IN HEART	394	*Marion*	ALVH
SING PRAISE TO GOD WHO REIGNS ABOVE	343	*Mit Freuden Zart*	
SOME CHILDREN SEE HIM	181	*Some Children*	
arr. Hawley Ades, "The Alfred Burt			
Christmas Carols," Shawnee Press, Inc., E77			
TEACH US WHAT WE YET MAY BE	9	*Hymn to Joy*	AOrl
THE CHURCH'S ONE FOUNDATION	547	*Aurelia*	ALVH
arr. John Ness Beck,			
"Upon This Rock," G. Schimer, Inc., 11467			
THE FIRST NOEL	179	*The First Noel*	ALVH, AOrl
arr. Ralph Vaughan Williams, Oxford, 46.509			
THE LORD'S MY SHEPHERD	42	*Brother James' Air*	AOrl
arr. Gordon Jacob,			
"Brother James' Air," Oxford, 43.902			
THEY'LL KNOW WE ARE CHRISTIANS			
BY OUR LOVE	677	*St. Brendan's*	AOrl
arr. Fred Bock,			
Fred Bock Music Company, B-G0133			
THINE IS THE GLORY	291	*Judas Maccabeus*	
THIS IS MY FATHER'S WORLD	6	*Terra Beata*	ALVH
arr. Buryl Red, Broadman Press, 4560-38			
WE GATHER TOGETHER	387	*Kremser*	
arr. John Ness Beck, Beckenhorst Press, BP1047			

TITLE	PAGE	TUNE	PERFORMANCE
WHAT CHILD IS THIS, WHO, LAID TO REST	180	*Greensleeves*	AOrl,
WHAT WONDROUS LOVE IS THIS?	283	*Wondrous Love*	U/with accompaniment
WHEN MORNING GILDS THE SKIES	322	*Laudes Domini*	ALVH
HOW GREAT OUR JOY	182	*Jungst*	AOrl, Echo choir
WHILE SHEPHERDS WATCHED THEIR FLOCKS	175	*Christmas*	AOrl

For additional hymntune choral arrangements see SATB Choral Selections Based on Hymns Found in *Hymns for the Family of God* page 98.

SATB Selections

BASED ON HYMNS FOUND IN
"HYMNS FOR THE FAMILY OF GOD"

Compiled by Fred Bock

FINDING GOOD, usable, singable anthems based on hymntunes is a difficult task. On one hand, there must be well over a million choral octavos from which to choose; but on the other hand, much of the time it seems that *nothing* is available! What we have attempted to provide in this listing is some handy information that will make the selection process easier. No doubt you will recognize titles, arrangers, or publishers whose names will be familiar territory to you. Some of the suggested arrangements are easy, some not-so-easy. All are SATB unless otherwise indicated. We have purposely left some space by those selections where we were unable to locate materials. Fill in those empty places as you find good anthems, and your book will be even more complete and functional for you.

Only separate octavo editions are included in this listing. Additional titles certainly are available in choral collections. Write to the various publishers listed in the back of this book for further information. Check also the listing by Lucy Hirt, *Children's Choral Materials Based on Hymns found in "Hymns for the Family of God."*

(All octavos are SATB unless otherwise indicated)

Title	Page #	Composer

A CHRISTIAN HOME
  see: A SONG OF PEACE, and
  BE STILL MY SOUL
	538	Jean Sibelius

A HYMN OF JOY WE SING	565	Mason and Webb's *Cantica Laudis*

A MIGHTY FORTRESS IS OUR GOD
  Caldwell, "God is in This Place,"
    Fred Bock Music Company B-G0316
  Mueller, G. Schirmer, 8179
  Simeone, Shawnee, A-349
	118	Martin Luther

Title	Page #	Composer
A SHELTER IN THE TIME OF STORM	117	Ira D. Sankey
A SONG OF PEACE Wood, Sacred Music Press, S41	682	Jean Sibelius
A WONDERFUL SAVIOR IS JESUS MY LORD see: HE HIDETH MY SOUL	120	
ABIDE WITH ME Hirt, Fred Bock Music Company, B-G0119 Kirk, Pro-Art, 1297 Wilson, Lorenz, 4429	500	William H. Monk
ALAS! AND DID MY SAVIOR BLEED Olds, Schmitt Music, 1862, (SATB&A solo)	274	Hugh Wilson
ALAS, AND DID MY SAVIOR BLEED see: AT THE CROSS	95	
ALL CREATURES OF OUR GOD AND KING Berglund, Beacon Hill, AN-6058 ———, Galaxy, 1.1882, (SSAATTBB)	347	*Geistliche Kirchengesang*
ALL FOR JESUS ———, Lorenz, A493	459	Unknown
ALL GLORY, LAUD AND HONOR Cain, Harold Flammer, A-5035 Douglas, Pro-Art, 2261 Fettke, Beacon Hill, AN-6033 Frackenpohl, E. B. Marks, 4245, (SATB&Jr. Choir) Olds, Carl Fischer, CM-600 (opt. 3 trp)	249	Melchior Teschner
ALL HAIL THE POWER OF JESUS' NAME (CORONATION) Dawson, Pro-Art, 1439 Gerig, Lillenas, AN-2372 (SSAATTBB) Hess, Singspiration, ZJP-3522 Simeone, Shawnee, A-783	325	Oliver Holden
ALL HAIL THE POWER OF JESUS' NAME (DIADEM) Ehret, Boston Music, 12908 Young, G., Presser, 312-40466	326	James Ellor
ALL HAIL THE POWER OF JESUS' NAME (MILES LANE) Cartford, Augsburg, 1113 Riegger, Harold Flammer, D-5128, (SAB) Ward, Harold Flammer, A-5011	327	William Shrubsole
ALL MY HEART TODAY REJOICES Lovelace, Hope, CH-650 (SAB)	203	Johann G. Ebeling
ALL MY LIFE LONG I HAD PANTED see: SATISFIED	100	

Title	Page #	Composer
ALL PEOPLE THAT ON EARTH DO DWELL see: PRAISE GOD FROM WHOM ALL BLESSINGS FLOW Johnson, Singspiration, ZJP-7255 Jolley, Lawson-Gould, 623	381	Louis Bourgeois
ALL POWER IS GIVEN UNTO ME see: FAR, FAR AWAY IN SIN AND DARKNESS DWELLING	674	
ALL PRAISE TO HIM WHO REIGNS ABOVE see: BLESSED BE THE NAME	352	
ALL PRAISE TO THEE, MY GOD Roesch, "Praise God Ye Servants," Harold Flammer, A-5682 Wienhorst, Concordia, 98-1791	518	Thomas Tallis
ALL THE WAY MY SAVIOR LEADS ME Burroughs, Word, CS-2634	598	Robert Lowry
ALL TO JESUS I SURRENDER see: I SURRENDER ALL	408	
ALL WILL BE WELL see: THROUGH THE LOVE OF GOD, OUR SAVIOR	498	
ALLELUIA Bock, "Praise Hymn," Fred Bock Music Company, B-G0306 Coates, Glory Sound, A-5756 Mickelson, Singspiration, ZJP-8195 Wyrtzen, Singspiration, ZJP-5052	361	Traditional Melody
ALMOST PERSUADED	437	Philip P. Bliss
AM I A SOLDIER OF THE CROSS? DeCou, Singspiration, ZJP-7216	411	Thomas A. Arne
AMAZING GRACE! HOW SWEET THE SOUND Beck, Beckenhorst, BP1004 Bock, Fred Bock Music Company, B-G0195 Coates, Shawnee, A-1130 Furnivall, Hinshaw, HMC-255 Hustad, Hope, HA-501 (SSAATTBB) Shaw/Parker, Lawson-Gould, 918	107	American Melody
AMERICA see: MY COUNTRY 'TIS OF THEE	695	
AMERICA, OUR HERITAGE Ades, Shawnee, A-225	694	Helen Steele
AMERICA, THE BEAUTIFUL Cross, Harold Flammer, A-5112 Johnson, Singspiration, ZJP-8214 Peery, Presser, 332-15134 Ringwald, Shawnee, A-158	690	Samuel A. Ward

Title	Page #	Composer
AND CAN IT BE THAT I SHOULD GAIN? Johnson, Singspiration, ZJP-7259	260	Thomas Campbell
ANGELS FROM THE REALMS OF GLORY Hastings, Bourne, HA5 Pooler, Augsburg, 1224, (SATB & Jr. Choir)	190	Henry T. Smart
ANGELS WE HAVE HEARD ON HIGH Christiansen, Augsburg, 1145, (SATB & treble choir) McKelvy, Mark Foster, MF 503 Peterson, Singspiration, ZJP-3014 Shaw/Parker, Lawson-Gould, 718 (5 part mixed choir) Wasner, G. Schirmer, 8564 Wilson, "Gloria In Excelsis Deo," Somerset, JW 7782	192	French Carol
ANYWHERE WITH JESUS DeCou, Singspiration, ZJP-6023	594	Daniel B. Towner
"ARE YE ABLE," SAID THE MASTER	470	Harry S. Mason
ARE YOU WASHED IN THE BLOOD?	259	Elisha A. Hoffman
AS WITH GLADNESS MEN OF OLD Johnson, Singspiration, ZJP-3010	202	Conrad Kocher
AT CALVARY Doig, Hope, GC 815 Peterson, Singspiration, ZJP-8002	415	Daniel B. Towner
AT THE CROSS	95	Ralph E. Hudson
AT THE NAME OF JESUS Johnson, Singspiration, ZJP-7317 Vaughan Williams, Oxford, 40.100	351	Ralph Vaughan Williams
AWAY IN A MANGER (AWAY IN A MANGER) Ehret, Sam Fox, CC10, (SAB) Hustad, Hope, A499 Long, Lillenas, AN-4019, (2pt. Jr. Choir) Ossewaarde, H. W. Gray, CMR-2665 Rotermund, Concordia, 98-1929	185	James R. Murray
AWAY IN A MANGER (CRADLE SONG) Brewer, Presser, 312-40617, (SATB & Jr. Choir) DeCou, Singspiration, ZJP-3008 Hustad, Hope, A499 Pooler, Augsburg, 1369, (unis treb choir & desc)	187	William J. Kirkpatrick
BATTLE HYMN OF THE REPUBLIC Burroughs, Lillenas, AN-3854 Ringwald, Shawnee, A-28 Wilhousky, Carl Fischer, CM-4743	692	American Melody
BE STILL MY SOUL Bish, Beckenhorst, BP1030 DeCou, Singspiration, ZJP-7287	77	Jean Sibelius

Title	Page #	Composer
BE NOT DISMAYED WHATE'ER BETIDE see: GOD WILL TAKE CARE OF YOU	56	
BE THOU MY VISION Ehret, Lillenas, AN-2418 Ehret, Lillenas, AN-2436, (SAB) Elrich, Manna, M-102 Godfrey, Presser, 332-15116 Johnson, Singspiration, ZJP-7331 Parker, Hinshaw, HML-135 Pooler, Augsburg, 1155, (SATB&Jr. Choir)	468	Traditional Irish Melody
BECAUSE HE LIVES Bock, "We Shall Live Because He Lives," Fred Bock Music Company, B-G0381 Gaither, Gaither Music, G-G5102 Huff, Gaither Music, G-G5108	292	William J. Gaither
BEGIN, MY TONGUE, SOME HEAVENLY THEME Young, Carl Fischer, CM-7786	328	Henry W. Greatorex' *Collection*
BENEATH THE CROSS OF JESUS	253	Frederick C. Maker
BEYOND THE SUNSET	127	Blanche Kerr Brock
BLESS HIS HOLY NAME Crouch, Lexicon, CS-2624	379	Andraé Crouch
BLESS THE LORD, O MY SOUL see: BLESS HIS HOLY NAME	379	
BLESSED ASSURANCE, JESUS IS MINE Kirk, Lillenas, AT-1022 Skiles, Lillenas, AN-1163 Wyrtzen, Singspiration, ZJP-5082	67	Phoebe P. Knapp
BLESSED BE THE NAME Johnson, Singspiration, ZJP-6018	352	Ralph E. Hudson
BLESSED JESUS	39	William J. Gaither
BLESSED QUIETNESS	145	W. S. Marshall
BLESSED REDEEMER Mercer, Benson, S-4050	275	Harry Dixon Loes
BLEST BE THE TIE THAT BINDS	560	Johann G. Naegeli
BREAK FORTH, O BEAUTEOUS HEAVENLY LIGHT Bach, Augsburg, 1055 Bach, E. C. Schirmer, 302 Bach-Lowden, Harold Flammer, D-5089, (SAB) Bach, Presser, 332-13744 Shaw/Parker, G. Schirmer, 10180	207	Johann Schop
BREAK THOU THE BREAD OF LIFE Lockwood, Southern, ———	30	William F. Sherwin

Title	Page #	Composer
BREATHE ON ME, BREATH OF GOD Kiser, Mark Foster, MF103	161	Robert Jackson
BRETHREN, WE HAVE MET TO WORSHIP Ehret, Lillenas, AN-2397 Johnson, Singspiration, ZJP-7276	321	William Moore
BUILT ON THE ROCK Brandon, Augsburg, 1416 Lundquist, Sam Fox, PS11 Rasley, Singspiration, ZJP-7279	555	Ludwig M. Lindeman
BURDENS ARE LIFTED AT CALVARY DeCou, Singspiration, ZJP-8093	60	John M. Moore
CALVARY COVERS IT ALL	250	Mrs. Walter G. Taylor
CAST THY BURDEN UPON THE LORD Mendelssohn, Carl Fischer, CM-6604 Mendelssohn, G. Schirmer, 10015 Mendelssohn, Kjos, 7003 Mendelssohn, Presser, 332-00825	53	Felix Mendelssohn
CHILD IN THE MANGER Bock, Fred Bock Music Company, B-G0278, (SAB) Douglas, Pro-Art, 2068	198	Traditional Gaelic Melody
CHILDREN OF THE HEAVENLY FATHER Christiansen, Schmitt, 912 Hustad, Hope, HA 101 Pooler, Harold Flammer, A-5123 Schneider, Harold Flammer, E-5057	89	Traditional Swedish Melody
CHRIST AROSE Johnson, N., Singspiration, ZJP-3540 Johnson, P., Word, CS-2871	298	Robert Lowry
CHRIST FOR THE WORLD WE SING	686	Felice de Giardini
CHRIST HAS FOR SIN ATONEMENT MADE see: WHAT A WONDERFUL SAVIOR	372	
CHRIST IS COMING!	303	William Owen
CHRIST IS MADE THE SURE FOUNDATION	557	Henry T. Smart
CHRIST RETURNETH! Mickelson, Singspiration, ZJP-8123 Skillings, Lillenas, AT-1087	304	James McGranahan
CHRIST THE LORD IS RISEN TODAY Carmichael, Lexicon, CS-2505 Huff, Paragon, P-PM35014 Peterson, Singspiration, ZJP-3517 Shaw/Parker, G. Schirmer, 9951 Vree, Carl Fischer, CM-7724	289	*"Lyra Davidica"*

Title	Page #	Composer
CHRIST, WE DO ALL ADORE THEE ———, G. Schirmer, 9749	358	Theodore Dubois
CHRIST WHOSE GLORY FILLS THE SKIES	293	Charles Gounod
CLEANSE ME Hustad, Hope, HA-122 Yarborough, Lillenas, AN-1174	425	Maori Melody
CLOSE TO THEE Mickelson, Singspiration, ZJP-8125	405	Silas J. Vail
COME, ALL CHRISTIANS, BE COMMITTED	507	*"The Sacred Harp"*
COME, CHRISTIANS, JOIN TO SING Linn, Lillenas, AN-2461 Mueller, Carl Fischer, CM-7470 Young, Hope, F954 (SATB & 2 trumpets)	342	Traditional
COME, EVERY SOUL BY SIN OPPRESSED see: ONLY TRUST HIM	629	
COME, HOLY SPIRIT Gaither, Gaither Music, G-G5109	150	William J. Gaither
COME, HOLY SPIRIT, DOVE DIVINE	559	H. Percy Smith
COME, HOLY SPIRIT, HEAVENLY DOVE	144	Johann Crüger
COME, THOU ALMIGHTY KING Howorth, Belwin-Mills, 1211 Thompson, V.D., "Hymn to the Trinity," Lorenz, 9578 Wiley, Pro-Art, 1361	341	Felice de Giardini
COME, THOU FOUNT OF EVERY BLESSING Cram, Carl Fischer, SIG. 113 DeCou, Singspiration, ZJP-7270 Wagner, Harold Flammer, A-5726	318	John Wyeth
COME, THOU LONG-EXPECTED JESUS	168	Rowland Hugh Prichard
COME TO CALVARY'S HOLY MOUNTAIN	276	Ludwig M. Lindeman
COME TO THE WATER see: FOR THOSE TEARS I DIED	436	
COME, WE THAT LOVE THE LORD	550	Robert Lowry
COME, YE SINNERS, POOR AND NEEDY	428	*"The Sacred Harp"*
COME, YE THANKFUL PEOPLE, COME Anthony, Singspiration, ZJP-3101 Ives, "Three Harvest Home Carols," Presser, 352-00361 Nelson, Augsburg, 1526	392	George J. Elvey

Title	Page #	Composer
COMING AGAIN	305	
see: JESUS IS COMING AGAIN		
CROWN HIM WITH MANY CROWNS	345	George J. Elvey
Cain, Harold Flammer, A-5016		
Hall, Lillenas, AN-2455		
Johnson, Augsburg, 1574		
Pelz, Augsburg, 9093		
Wilson, Hope, F909, (SATB& brass)		
Wyrtzen, Singspiration, ZJP-3548		
DAY BY DAY AND WITH EACH PASSING MOMENT	102	Oscar Ahnfelt
Johnson, Singspiration, ZJP-7350		
DAYS ARE FILLED WITH SORROW AND CARE	60	
see: BURDENS ARE LIFTED AT CALVARY		
DEAR LORD AND FATHER OF MANKIND	422	Frederick C. Maker
Larson, Pro-Art, 1139		
Olds, Schmitt, 1870		
Peery, Presser, 312-40427		
DOWN AT THE CROSS	255	John H. Stockton
DOXOLOGY	382,384	Louis Bourgeois
Bock, "Praise God," Lorenz, S-113		
DRAW ME NEARER	455	
see: I AM THINE, O LORD		
DYING WITH JESUS, BY DEATH RECKONED MINE	65	
see: MOMENT BY MOMENT		
EARTH AND ALL STARS	10	David N. Johnson
EARTHLY FRIENDS MAY PROVE UNTRUE	651	
see: JESUS NEVER FAILS		
ENCAMPED ALONG THE HILLS OF LIGHT	71	
see: FAITH IS THE VICTORY		
ETERNAL FATHER, STRONG TO SAVE	679	John Bacchus Dykes
Treharne, Boston, 10310		
ETERNAL LIFE	474	Olive Dungan
Bock, Presser, 322-40042		
Stickles, Presser, 322-40018		
EVEN SO, LORD JESUS, COME	429	William J. Gaither
Gaither, Gaither Music, G-G5110		
Huff, Paragon, P-PM35017		
FACE TO FACE	128	Grant C. Tullar

Title	Page #	Composer
FAIREST LORD JESUS Christiansen, F.M., "Beautiful Savior," Augsburg, 1447 Gillette, Summy, 1393 Hustad, Hope, HA 102, (SAB)	240	Silesian Folk Melody
FAITH IS THE VICTORY	71	Ira D. Sankey
FAITH OF OUR FATHERS Johnson, Singspiration, ZJP-6005 Mann, Lexicon, CS-2720 Ringwald, Shawnee, A-77	526	Henri F. Hemy
FAR AWAY IN THE DEPTHS OF MY SPIRIT see: WONDERFUL PEACE	494	
FAR, FAR AWAY IN SIN AND DARKNESS DWELLING	674	James McGranahan
FATHER, I ADORE YOU	414	Terrye Coelho
FEAR NOT, LITTLE FLOCK, FROM THE CROSS see: ONLY BELIEVE	585	
FIGHT THE GOOD FIGHT	613	William Boyd
FILL ME NOW	153	John R. Sweney
FILL MY CUP, LORD Burroughs, Word, CS-2500	481	Richard Blanchard
FILL THOU MY LIFE, O LORD MY GOD	479	Thomas Haweis
FOR ALL THE SAINTS Shaw, G. Schirmer, 9908 Vaughan Williams, Carl Fischer, CM-6637	614	Ralph Vaughan Williams
FOR GOD SO LOVED THE WORLD	315	Alfred B. Smith
FOR THE BEAUTY OF THE EARTH Chenoweth, Lawson-Gould, 51397 DeCou, Singspiration, ZJP-3107 Gerig, Lillenas, AN-2383 Shaw, G. Schirmer, 10097	1	Conrad Kocher
FOR THOSE TEARS I DIED Wilson, Hope, CF 195	436	Marsha Stevens
FOR YOU I AM PRAYING see: I AM PRAYING FOR YOU	676	
GENTLE SHEPHERD Powell, Gaither Music, G-G5122	596	William J. Gaither
GET ALL EXCITED Bock, Gaither Music, G-G5127 Gaither, Gaither Music, G-G5112	652	William J. Gaither
GETTING USED TO THE FAMILY OF GOD ———, Gaither Music, G-G5135	548	William J. Gaither

Title	Page #	Composer
GIVE OF YOUR BEST TO THE MASTER	516	Charlotte A. Barnard
GLAD DAY! GLAD DAY! see: IS IT THE CROWNING DAY?	310	
GLORIA PATRI Wilson, Hope, AG-7214	142	Henry W. Greatorex
GLORIOUS IS THY NAME, MOST HOLY	510	William Moore
GLORIOUS THINGS OF THEE ARE SPOKEN DeCou, Singspiration, ZJP-7254 Ehret, Carl Fischer, CM-7117 Harris, L., Word, CS-2892 Shaw/Parker, Lawson-Gould, 756 Smith, Lillenas, AN-2355	376	Franz Joseph Haydn
GLORY BE TO THE FATHER see: GLORIA PATRI	142	
GLORY TO HIS NAME see: DOWN AT THE CROSS	255	
GO, TELL IT ON THE MOUNTAINS Barthelson, Belwin-Mills 2050 DeCou, Singspiration, ZJP-3029 Krasser, Carl Fischer, CM-6908 Ridenour, Hope, SP 743, (2 parts) Simeone, Shawnee, A-482 Sjolund, Word, CS-2406	205	Traditional American Song
GO TO DARK GETHSEMANE	281	Richard Redhead
GOD BE WITH YOU 'TIL WE MEET AGAIN	523	William G. Tomer
GOD IS AT WORK WITHIN YOU Bock, Fred Bock Music Company, B-G0117, (2 parts)	584	Fred Bock
GOD LEADS US ALONG Floyd, Hope, F-1 Nelson, Sacred Manuscripts, V-104	597	G. A. Young
GOD MOVES IN A MYSTERIOUS WAY	603	*Scottish Psalter*
GOD OF GRACE AND GOD OF GLORY Burroughs, Lillenas, AN-2328	528	John Hughes
GOD OF OUR FATHERS Bish, Beckenhorst, BP1062 Davies, Harold Flammer, A-5452 Gearhart, Shawnee, A-111 Hustad, Hope, F-922, (brass choir opt) Johnson, Singspiration, ZJP-7288 Pollack, World Library Publications, ESA-1904-8	687	George W. Warren
GOD SENT HIS SON see: BECAUSE HE LIVES	292	

Title	Page #	Composer
GOD SO LOVED THE WORLD Page, Carl Fischer, CM-283 Stainer, Augsburg, 1038 Stainer, G. Schirmer, 3798 Stainer, Presser, 332-08621	20	John Stainer
GOD THE OMNIPOTENT Lundberg, Singspiration, ZJP-7307	353	Alexis F. Lvov
GOD, WHO MADE THE EARTH AND HEAVEN Ehret, Hope, JR-202 (SA)	4	Traditional Welsh Melody
GOD, WHO STRETCHED THE SPANGLED HEAVENS see: TEACH US WHAT WE YET MAY BE	9	
GOD, WHOSE GIVING KNOWS NO ENDING	513	John Wyeth
GOD WILL TAKE CARE OF YOU	56	W. Stillman Martin
GOD CHRISTIAN MEN, REJOICE Bennett, Lawson-Gould, Many Moods of Christmas Gordon, Presser, 312-40231 Johnson, Singspiration, ZJP-3006 Shaw/Parker, G. Schirmer, 10183 Terri, Lawson-Gould, 678 Wilson, Hope, CH-640	177	German Melody
GRACE GREATER THAN OUR SIN Gerig, Hope, GC-813 Hustad, Hope, HA 111 Kaiser, "Marvelous Hope," Hope, GC-809	105	Daniel B. Towner
GREAT GOD OF WONDERS!	104	John Newton
GREAT GOD, WE SING YOUR MIGHTY HAND	7	William Gardiner's *Sacred Melodies*
GREAT HILLS MAY TREMBLE AND MOUNTAINS see: SECURITY	496	
GREAT IS THY FAITHFULNESS Bock, Hope, TB-201, (TTBB) Hustad, Hope, HA-113	98	William M. Runyan
GUIDE ME, O THOU GREAT JEHOVAH Burroughs, Lillenas, AN-2379 Coggin, Pro-Art, 2541 Hustad, Hope, HA-114	608	John Hughes
HALLELUJAH, WHAT A SAVIOR! see: "MAN OF SORROWS," WHAT A NAME!	246	
HAPPY THE HOME WHEN GOD IS THERE	540	John B. Dykes

Title	Page #	Composer
HARK! THE HERALD ANGELS SING DeCou, Singspiration, ZJP-3007 Nagel, Lillenas, AN-3884 Shaw/Parker, Lawson-Gould, 728 Swift, Pro-Art, 1289 Williamson, Fred Bock Music Company, B-G0288	184	Felix Mendelssohn
HAVE THINE OWN WAY, LORD! Hustad, Hope, HA-116 Landon, Lorenz, A-375	400	George C. Stebbins
HAVE YOU ANY ROOM FOR JESUS? Williams, Lorenz, A301	654	C. C. Williams
HAVE YOU BEEN TO JESUS see: ARE YOU WASHED IN THE BLOOD?	259	
HE GIVETH MORE GRACE Mickelson, Lillenas AN-1155 Widen, Lillenas AN-1703	112	Hubert Mitchell
HE HIDETH MY SOUL Ferrin, Lillenas, AN-1642 Warford, Word, CS-2604	120	William J. Kirkpatrick
HE KEEPS ME SINGING Carmichael, Lexicon, CS-2484	587	Luther B. Bridgers
HE IS LORD	234	Traditional
HE LEADETH ME, O BLESSED THOUGHT Cain, Harold Flammer, A-5489 Stanislaw, Lillenas, AN-1655	606	William B. Bradbury
HE LEFT THE SPLENDOR OF HEAVEN see: IF THAT ISN'T LOVE	224	
HE LIFTED ME	653	Charles H. Gabriel
HE LIVES Roe, Word, CS-2305	299	Alfred H. Ackley
HE THE PEARLY GATES WILL OPEN Johnson, Singspiration, ZJP-8025 Skiles, Lillenas, AN-1127	72	Elsie Ahlwen
HE TOUCHED ME Gaither, Gaither Music, G-G5103 Powell, Gaither Music, G-G5130	628	William J. Gaither
HE'S EVERYTHING TO ME Carmichael, Lexicon, CS-321	632	Ralph Carmichael
HE'S STILL THE KING OF KINGS Huff, Gaither Music, G-G5114 Lane, Gaither Music, G-G5104	242	William J. Gaither

Title	Page #	Composer
HE'S THE SAVIOR OF MY SOUL	247	Spanish Melody
HEAR THE BELLS RINGING	301	
see: THE EASTER SONG		
HEAR THE VOICE OF JESUS CALLING	669	Gregorian Chant
HEAVEN CAME DOWN AND GLORY FILLED MY SOUL	657	John W. Peterson
Collins, Lillenas, AT-1039		
DeCou, Singspiration, ZJP-8017		
Hustad, Hope, GC-804		
HERE, O MY LORD, I SEE THEE FACE TO FACE	567	Edward Dearle
HIDING IN THEE	70	Ira. D. Sankey
HIGHER GROUND	469	Charles H. Gabriel
Linn, Lillenas, AT-1126		
HIS NAME IS WONDERFUL	230	Audrey Mieir
Bolks, Manna, M-128		
HOLY BIBLE, BOOK DIVINE	34	William B. Bradbury
HOLY GHOST, WITH LIGHT DIVINE	162	Louis M. Gottschalk
HOLY GOD, WE PRAISE THY NAME	385	*Allgemeines*
Hustad, Hope, F-904		*Katholisches*
Johnson, Singspiration, ZJP-7337		*Gesangbuch*
Peloquin, Summy, 2267		
HOLY, HOLY	149	Jimmy Owens
Owens, Lexicon, CS-2167		
HOLY! HOLY! HOLY! LORD GOD ALMIGHTY	323	John B. Dykes
Beck, "A Holy Festival," Fred Bock Music		
Company, B-G0181,		
(SATB & Childrens Choir & Cong.)		
Gilbert, Harold Flammer, D-5096 (SAB)		
Johnson, Singspiration, ZJP-6040		
Ringwald, Shawnee A-36		
Townsend, Pro-Art, 1321		
HOLY SPIRIT, FLOW THROUGH ME	164	Walt Mills
HOSANNA, LOUD HOSANNA	248	*Gesangbüch der*
Wilson, Hope, F-910 (SATB & Jr. Choir)		*Herzogl, Wirtemberg*
HOVER O'ER ME, HOLY SPIRIT	153	
see: FILL ME NOW		
HOW CAN I SAY THANKS	365	
see: MY TRIBUTE		
HOW FIRM A FOUNDATION	32	Traditional
Krogstad, Singspiration, ZJP-6038		American Melody
Niles, G. Schirmer, 11313		
Skillings, Lillenas, AN-1162		
Young, Harold Flammer, A-5599		

Title	Page #	Composer
HOW GREAT OUR JOY! Jungst, "While By My Sheep," Plymouth, XM-114 Jungst, Harold Flammer, A-5086	182	Traditional German Melody
HOW GREAT THOU ART Bock, Fred Bock Music Company, B-G0161 Bock, Fred Bock Music Company, B-G0162, (SAB) Elrich, Manna, M-123 Mickelson, Manna, M-2	2	Stuart K. Hine
HOW MARVELOUS! HOW WONDERFUL! see: I STAND AMAZED	223	
HOW SWEET THE NAME OF JESUS SOUNDS	229	Alexander R. Reinagle
HYMN TO THE TRINITY Sjolund, "Responses for Worship," Word, CS-665	140	Paul Sjolund
I AM HIS AND HE IS MINE Gassman, Word, CS-2804 Thomas, Lillenas, AN-1731	590	James Mountain
I AM NOT SKILLED TO UNDERSTAND	94	Cecil J. Allen
I AM PRAYING FOR YOU Soderwall, Manna, M-203	676	Ira D. Sankey
I AM SO GLAD THAT MY FATHER IN HEAVEN see: JESUS LOVES EVEN ME	225	
I AM THINE, O LORD	455	William H. Doane
I AM TRUSTING THEE, LORD JESUS	73	Ethelbert W. Bullinger
I BELIEVE IN A HILL CALLED MOUNT CALVARY ____, Gaither Music, G-G5136	270	William J. Gaither
I CAN HEAR MY SAVIOR CALLING see: WHERE HE LEADS ME	607	
I CANNOT TELL	210	Traditional Irish Melody
I COME TO THE GARDEN ALONE see: IN THE GARDEN	588	
I COULD NEVER OUTLOVE THE LORD ____, Gaither Music, G-5137	452	William J. Gaither
I HAVE A SAVIOR, HE'S PLEADING IN GLORY see: I AM PRAYING FOR YOU	676	
I HAVE A SONG I LOVE TO SING see: SINCE I HAVE BEEN REDEEMED	644	
I HAVE A SONG THAT JESUS GAVE ME see: IN MY HEART THERE RINGS A MELODY	633	

Title	Page #	Composer
I HEAR THE SAVIOR SAY see: JESUS PAID IT ALL	273	
I HEARD AN OLD, OLD STORY see: VICTORY IN JESUS	82	
I HEARD THE VOICE OF JESUS SAY Wiley, Pro-Art, 1860	51	John B. Dykes
I KNOW A FOUNT	265	Oliver Cooke
I KNOW NOT WHY GOD'S WONDROUS GRACE see: I KNOW WHOM I HAVE BELIEVED	631	
I KNOW THAT MY REDEEMER LIVES	295	John Hatton
I KNOW WHO HOLDS TOMORROW Kirk, Lillenas, AT-1059	96	Ira F. Stanphill
I KNOW WHOM I HAVE BELIEVED Ferrin, Lillenas, AN-1635	631	James McGranahan
I LAY MY SINS ON JESUS	427	Traditional Greek Melody
I LOVE TO TELL THE STORY	619	William G. Fischer
I LOVE YOUR KINGDOM, LORD	545	Williams' *New Universal Psalmodist*
I MUST TELL JESUS	49	Elisha A. Hoffman
I NEED JESUS	450	Charles H. Gabriel
I NEED THEE EVERY HOUR Beck, Beckenhorst, BP1067	443	Robert Lowry
I SERVE A RISEN SAVIOR see: HE LIVES	299	
I STAND AMAZED	223	Charles H. Gabriel
I SURRENDER ALL	408	Winfield S. Weeden
I THINK, WHEN I READ THAT SWEET STORY	213	William B. Bradbury
I WILL PRAISE HIM! Ulrich, Manna, M-157	359	Margaret J. Harris
I WILL SERVE THEE ____, Gaither Music, G-G5138	397	William J. Gaither
I WILL SING OF MY REDEEMER	228	James McGranahan
I WILL SING THE WONDROUS STORY	618	Peter P. Bilhorn
I WONDER AS I WANDER Niles/Horton, G. Schirmer, 8708	183	Traditional Appalachian Folksong
I'D RATHER HAVE JESUS Shea, Chancel Music, #101	650	George Beverly Shea

Title	Page #	Composer
I'LL BE THERE	130	Tim Spencer
I'LL GO WHERE YOU WANT ME TO GO	502	Carrie E. Rounsefell
I'LL LIVE FOR HIM	453	C. R. Dunbar
I'LL TELL THE WORLD THAT I'M A CHRISTIAN Bock, Fox Publications, B-G0229, (TTBB) Ehret, Fox Publications, B-G0257, (SAB) Huff, Fox Publications, B-G0189	648	Baynard L. Fox
I'M PRESSING ON THE UPWARD WAY see: HIGHER GROUND	469	
I'VE ANCHORED MY SOUL see: THE HAVEN OF REST	101	
I'VE FOUND A FRIEND, O SUCH A FRIEND Lovelace, Hope, CH655	220	George C. Stebbins
I'VE HAD MANY TEARS AND SORROWS see: THROUGH IT ALL	43	
I'VE WANDERED FAR AWAY FROM GOD see: LORD, I'M COMING HOME	406	
IF I GAINED THE WORLD	642	Traditional Swedish Melody
IF MY PEOPLE WILL PRAY Ownes, Lexicon, CS-2631	575	Jimmy Owens
IF THAT ISN'T LOVE Linn, Lillenas, AT-1139 Rambo, Benson, S-4148	224	Dottie Rambo
IF YOU WILL ONLY LET GOD GUIDE YOU Thompson, "If Thou But Suffer God to Guide Thee," Presser, 312-40105	605	Georg Neumark
IMMORTAL, INVISIBLE, GOD ONLY WISE Leupold, Augsburg, 1440 Young, Hope, CY-3344, (SAB)	319	Traditional Welsh Melody
IN A TIME OF TROUBLE See: THE HIDING PLACE	37	
IN CHRIST THERE IS NO EAST OR WEST Gassman, Lexicon, 37534 (Cantata)	685	Alexander R. Reinagle
IN HEAVEN ABOVE Christiansen, Augsburg, 0106	131	Traditional Norwegian Melody
IN LOVING-KINDNESS JESUS CAME see: HE LIFTED ME	653	
IN MY HEART THERE RINGS A MELODY Blakley, Hope, F2 Landon, Lorenz, A387	633	Elton M. Roth

Title	Page #	Composer
IN SHADY GREEN PASTURES see: GOD LEADS US ALONG	597	
IN THE CIRCLE OF EACH HOME Bock, Fred Bock Music Company, B-G0407	535	Bryan Jeffery Leech
IN THE CROSS OF CHRIST I GLORY Burkwall, Singspiration, ZJP-7302	251	Ithamar Conkey
IN THE GARDEN Boersma, Word, CS-2342	588	C. Austin Miles
IN THE HOUR OF TRIAL	122	Spencer Lane
IN THE STARS HIS HANDIWORK I SEE see: HE'S EVERYTHING TO ME	632	
INFANT HOLY, INFANT LOWLY Willcocks, Oxford, 84.123 Young, Hope, AG 7183	194	Traditional Polish Carol
IS IT THE CROWNING DAY?	310	Charles H. Marsh
IS MY NAME WRITTEN THERE?	125	Frank M. Davis
IS YOUR BURDEN HEAVY see: REACH OUT TO JESUS	430	
IT CAME UPON THE MIDNIGHT CLEAR Stone, Pro-Art, 1300	197	Richard S. Willis
IT IS GOOD TO SING THY PRAISES	330	Wolfgang A. Mozart
IT IS NO SECRET Ehret, MCA, VC 246, (SAB) Kerr, MCA, VC 720 Walton, MCA, VC 340	581	Stuart Hamblen
IT IS WELL WITH MY SOUL Rasley, Singspiration, ZJP-8105	495	Philip P. Bliss
IT MAY BE AT MORN see: CHRIST RETURNETH!	304	
IT MAY NOT BE ON THE MOUNTAIN'S HEIGHT see: I'LL GO WHERE YOU WANT ME TO GO	502	
IT ONLY TAKES A SPARK see: PASS IT ON	641	
IT TOOK A MIRACLE	626	John W. Peterson
IT WILL BE WORTH IT ALL	129	Esther Kerr Rusthoi
IT WILL BE WORTH IT ALL see: WHEN WE SEE CHRIST	135	William J. Gaither
JESUS CALLS US O'ER THE TUMULT Olds, Schmitt, 1860	399	William H. Jude

Title	Page #	Composer
JESUS CHRIST IS RISEN TODAY	297	Robert Williams
JESUS, I AM RESTING, RESTING	86	James Mountain
JESUS, I COME	401	George C. Stebbins
JESUS IS ALL THE WORLD TO ME Ferrin, Lillenas, AN-1614	627	Will L. Thompson
JESUS IS CALLING	434	George C. Stebbins
JESUS IS COMING AGAIN Mickelson, Singspiration, ZJP-8139	305	John W. Peterson
JESUS IS COMING TO EARTH AGAIN see: WHAT IF IT WERE TODAY?	311	
JESUS IS LORD OF ALL Powell, Gaither Music, G-G5123	235	William J. Gaither
JESUS IS TENDERLY CALLING YOU HOME see: JESUS IS CALLING	434	
JESUS IS THE FRIEND OF SINNERS	219	John W. Peterson
JESUS, KEEP ME NEAR THE CROSS see: NEAR THE CROSS	254	
JESUS LIVES, AND SO SHALL I	288	Johann Crüger
JESUS, LOVER OF MY SOUL Berglund, Beacon Hill, AN-6026	222	Joseph Parry
JESUS LOVES EVEN ME Williams, Hope, GC-820	225	Philip P. Bliss
JESUS LOVES ME, THIS I KNOW Bock, "Jesus Knows Me, and This I Love," Fox Publications, B-G0379	226	William B. Bradbury
JESUS LOVES THE LITTLE CHILDREN	15	George F. Root
JESUS MAY COME TODAY see: IS IT THE CROWNING DAY?	310	
JESUS MY LORD WILL LOVE ME FOREVER see: NOW I BELONG TO JESUS	637	
JESUS NEVER FAILS	651	Arthur A. Luther
JESUS PAID IT ALL Burroughs, Presser, 312-40988 Rasley, Singspiration, ZJP-7361	273	John T. Grape
JESUS, PRICELESS TREASURE Bach, Harold Flammer, A-5169 Ehret, E. B. Marks, 4112	277	Johann Crüger
JESUS SAVES! Crill, Lillenas, AN-1103	667	William Kirkpatrick

Title	Page #	Composer
JESUS SHALL REIGN WHERE'ER THE SUN Bock, Fred Bock Music Company, B-G0249 Boersma, Word, CS-2382 Ibbotson, Harold Flammer, A-5249	238	John Hatton
JESUS, THE SON OF GOD	269	G. T. Haywood
JESUS, THE VERY THOUGHT OF THEE Carmichael, Lexicon, CS-306 Olds, Schmitt, 1866 Walton, Boosey & Hawkes, 5143	465	John B. Dykes
JESUS, THOU JOY OF LOVING HEARTS Swift, Boosey & Hawkes, 1981	451	Henry Baker
JESUS, THY BLOOD AND RIGHTEOUSNESS	268	William Gardiner's *Sacred Melodies*
JESUS WALKED THIS LONESOME VALLEY Kirk, Pro-Art, 2004 Wilson/Ehret, Boosey & Hawkes, 1936	217	Traditional Spiritual
JESUS, WE JUST WANT TO THANK YOU Bock, Gaither Music, G-G5133	461	William J. Gaither
JESUS! WHAT A FRIEND FOR SINNERS	244	Rowland Hugh Prichard
JESUS WILL WALK WITH ME	609	Haldor Lillenas
JOIN ALL THE GLORIOUS NAMES Wytzen, Singspiration, ZJP-7341	232	John Darwall
JOY OF THE LORD see: THE JOY OF THE LORD	354	
JOY TO THE WORLD! Bock, Fred Bock Music Company, B-G0180 Carmichael, Lexicon, CS-2683 Johnson, Singspiration, ZJP-3034 Shaw/Parker, Lawson-Gould, 712	171	George Friedrich Handel
JOYFUL, JOYFUL, WE ADORE THEE Angell, Plymouth, HA-1 Keene, Lillenas, AN-2449 McCall, Singspiration, ZJP-6019 Sanders, Presser, 332-14893 Simeone, Shawnee, A 781	377	Ludwig van Beethoven
JOYS ARE FLOWING LIKE A RIVER see: BLESSED QUIETNESS	145	
JUST A CLOSER WALK WITH THEE Elrich, Glory Sound, A-5792 Rasley, Singspiration, ZJP-8211 Wilson, Hope, HO 1809 ——Lorenz, A406	591	Traditional American Folk Song

Title	Page #	Composer
JUST AS I AM, WITHOUT ONE PLEA	417	William B. Bradbury
KIND AND MERCIFUL GOD	419	Traditional Swedish Melody
KING OF MY LIFE I CROWN THEE NOW see: LEAD ME TO CALVARY	407	
LEAD ME TO CALVARY Hustad, Hope, HA 117	407	William J. Kirkpatrick
LEAD ON, O KING ETERNAL Byles, G. Schirmer, 10855 Gerig, Lillenas, AN-2292	595	Henry T. Smart
LEANING ON THE EVERLASTING ARMS Drevits, Singspiration, ZJP-8114 Skiles, Lillenas, AN-1160	87	Anthony J. Showalter
LET ALL MORTAL FLESH KEEP SILENCE Diggle, G. Schirmer, 10005 Grieb, G. Schirmer, 10516 Rasley, Singspiration, ZJP-7272 Vance, Belwin-Mills, 2209 Young, C., Hope, AG-7156	166	Traditional French Carol
LET ALL THINGS NOW LIVING Davis, K. K., E. C. Schirmer, #1770 Glaser, E. C. Schirmer, #2476	389	Traditional Welsh Melody
LET GOD BE GOD Bock, Fred Bock Music Company, B-G0362	81	Bryan Jeffery Leech
LET JESUS COME INTO YOUR HEART Ferrin, Crescendo, 271	433	Lelia N. Morris
LET THERE BE PEACE ON EARTH Ades, Shawnee, A626	681	Sy Miller, Jill Jackson
LET US BREAK BREAD TOGETHER Beck, Hope A-447 Bock, "Four Communion Hymns," Hope A-450 Cain, Harold Flammer, A-5078 Ringwald, Shawnee Press, A-726 Sateren, Augsburg, 1143 Wilson/Ehret, Boosey & Hawkes, 5008	564	Traditional American Melody
LET US CELEBRATE THE GLORIES OF OUR LORD Bock, Fred Bock Music Company, B-G0364	320	Jean Joseph Mouret
LET YOUR HEART BE BROKEN Bock, Fred Bock Music Company, B-G0408	662	Bryan Jeffery Leech
LET'S JUST PRAISE THE LORD Powell, Gaither Music, G-G5115	317	William J. Gaither
LIFT UP YOUR HEADS, YE MIGHTY GATES Lynn, Presser, MC 220	239	*Psalmodia Evangelica*

Title	Page #	Composer
LIKE A LAMB WHO NEEDS THE SHEPHERD	61	Ralph Carmichael
LIKE A RIVER GLORIOUS Bock, Fred Bock Music Company, B-G0405 Burroughs, Presser, 312-41030 DeCou, Singspiration, ZJP-7340	497	James Mountain
LIKE THE WOMAN AT THE WELL see: FILL MY CUP, LORD	481	
LITTLE IS MUCH, WHEN GOD IS IN IT Huff, Paragon, PM-35019	512	Kittie Louise Suffield
LIVING FOR JESUS Jones, Word, CS-2059 Wilson, Lorenz, A-364	462	C. Harold Lowden
LO! HE COMES WITH CLOUDS DESCENDING	306	Henry T. Smart
LO! HOW A ROSE E'ER BLOOMING Bish, Beckenhorst Press, BP-1033 Distler, Concordia, 97-4849 Shaw/Parker, Lawson-Gould, 730	174	Michael Praetorius
LONG YEARS AGO see: THE STAR CAROL	201	
LORD, DISMISS US WITH YOUR BLESSING	520	Tattersall's *Psalmody*
LORD, I CARE NOT FOR RICHES see: IS MY NAME WRITTEN THERE?	125	
LORD, I WANT TO BE A CHRISTIAN Martin, Presser, 312-40082	421	Traditional American Melody
LORD, I'M COMING HOME	406	William J. Kirkpatrick
LORD JESUS, I LONG TO BE PERFECTLY WHOLE see: WHITER THAN SNOW	109	
LORD, MAKE ME AN INSTRUMENT OF THY PEACE see: ETERNAL LIFE	474	
LORD, SPEAK TO ME	625	Robert Schumann
LORD, WE PRAISE YOU Skillings, "Celebration of Praise" Lillenas, AN-2396	367	Otis Skillings
LOVE DIVINE, ALL LOVES EXCELLING Cain, Harold Flammer, A-5132	21	John Zundel
LOVE DIVINE, SO GREAT AND WONDROUS see: HE THE PEARLY GATES WILL OPEN	72	
LOVE SENT MY SAVIOR TO DIE IN MY STEAD see: WHY SHOULD HE LOVE ME SO?	26	

Title	Page #	Composer
LOVE WAS WHEN Wyrtzen, Singspiration, ZJP-5026	28	Don Wyrtzen
LOVED WITH EVERLASTING LOVE see: I AM HIS AND HE IS MINE	590	
LOW IN THE GRAVE HE LAY see: CHRIST AROSE	298	
MACEDONIA	668	Henry S. Cutler
MAKE ME A BLESSING	473	George S. Schuler
"MAN OF SORROWS," WHAT A NAME!	246	Philip P. Bliss
MARVELOUS GRACE OF OUR LOVING LORD see: GRACE GREATER THAN OUR SIN	105	
MARVELOUS MESSAGE WE BRING see: JESUS IS COMING AGAIN	305	
MAY THE MIND OF CHRIST, MY SAVIOR	483	Cyril Barham-Gould
MINE EYES HAVE SEEN THE GLORY see: BATTLE HYMN OF THE REPUBLIC	692	
MOMENT BY MOMENT	65	May W. Moody
MORE ABOUT JESUS WOULD I KNOW	477	John R. Sweney
MORE LOVE TO THEE, O CHRIST	476	William H. Doane
MORNING HAS BROKEN Powell, Word, CS-2587 Simeone, Shawnee, A-1175	5	Traditional Gaelic Melody
MUST JESUS BEAR THE CROSS ALONE	504	George N. Allen
MY COUNTRY, 'TIS OF THEE Hunter, "America," Carl Fischer, CM-7947	695	Henry Carey
MY FAITH HAS FOUND A RESTING PLACE Soderwall, Manna, M-188 Thomas, Lillenas, AN-2431	75	Traditional Norwegian Melody
MY FAITH LOOKS UP TO THEE Olds, Schmitt Music, 1868	84	Lowell Mason
MY HOPE IS BUILT see: THE SOLID ROCK	92	
MY HOPE IS IN THE LORD	78	Norman J. Clayton
MY JESUS, I LOVE THEE Eleiott, Lillenas, AT-1018	456	Adoniram J. Gordon
MY LORD, WHAT A MORNING! Barthelson, E. B. Marks, 4011 Page, Hinshaw, HMC-266 Wilson, Jack Spratt Music, 219 Work, Presser, 312-40622	316	Traditional Spiritual

Title	Page #	Composer
MY SAVIOR'S LOVE see: I STAND AMAZED	223	
MY SHEPHERD WILL SUPPLY MY NEED Johnson, Lillenas, AN-8010 Thomson, H. W. Gray, CMR 2046	66	Traditional Melody
MY TRIBUTE Crouch, Lexicon Music, CS-2625	365	Andraé Crouch
MY WONDERFUL LORD	368	Haldor Lillenas
NEAR THE CROSS McCall, Pro-Art, 2605	254	William H. Doane
NEAR TO THE HEART OF GOD Carmichael, Lexicon, CS-308 Ferguson, Lillenas, AN-2426	35	Cleland B. McAfee
NEARER, STILL NEARER	485	Lelia N. Morris
NO, NOT ONE! Crouch/Elrich, Manna, M-180 Linn, Lillenas, AT-1013	221	George C. Hugg
NO ONE UNDERSTANDS LIKE JESUS LaRowe, Word, CS-2338	36	John W. Peterson
NOTHING BUT THE BLOOD	266	Robert Lowry
NOW I BELONG TO JESUS ———, Lorenz, A-474	637	Norman J. Clayton
NOW THANK WE ALL OUR GOD Bach, H. W. Gray, CMR 1497 Frackenpohl, Shawnee, A-460 Hamill, Harold Flammer, D-5032 Shaw/Parker, Lawson-Gould, 753 Smart, Hope, F-906 (unison, tpt)	525	Johann Crüger
O BEAUTIFUL FOR SPACIOUS SKIES see: AMERICA, THE BEAUTIFUL	690	
O BREATH OF LIFE	579	Joel Blomqvist
O COME, ALL YE FAITHFUL Frazier, Beckenhorst, BP1025 Linn, Lillenas, AN-3870 Normand, Plymouth, XM-108 Peterson, Singspiration, ZJP-3009 Porter, Jack Spratt Music, 301	193	John F. Wade's *Cantus Diversi*
O COME, O COME, EMMANUEL Berglund, Beacon Hill, AN-6046 Christiansen, Augsburg, 1085 Goodwin, Harold Flammer, A-5057 Johnson, Singspiration, ZJP-3003 Kirk, Pro-Art, 1645 Lynn, Presser, MC 217	169	Plainsong

Title	Page #	Composer
O COULD I SPEAK THE MATCHLESS WORTH	344	Wolfgang A. Mozart
O DAY OF REST AND GLADNESS DeCou, Singspiration, ZJP-7261 Stuart, Pro-Art, 1657	12	Traditional German Melody
O FOR A HEART TO PRAISE MY GOD	357	Thomas Haweis
O FOR A THOUSAND TONGUES TO SING Beck, Fred Bock Music Company, B-G0308 Carmichael, Lexicon, CS-305 Glaser, Carl Fischer, CM-7424 Schubert, Lillenas, AN-2395	349	Carl G. Glaser
O GIVE US HOMES BUILT FIRM UPON THE SAVIOR see: A CHRISTIAN HOME	538	
O GOD, OUR HELP IN AGES PAST Bolks, Singspiration, ZJP-7240 Butler, McAfee Music, M1119 Christiansen, Augsburg, 1213 Koehler/Ormsby, Bourne, 784 Martin, Presser, 332-40115	370	William Croft
O HAPPY DAY!	647	Edward F. Rimbault
O HOW HE LOVES YOU AND ME Huff, Paragon, P-PM 35018 Kaiser, Word, CS-2717	622	Kurt Kaiser
O HOW I LOVE JESUS Rasley, Singspiration, ZJP-8216	634	Traditional American Melody
O JESUS, I HAVE PROMISED	402	Arthur H. Mann
O LET YOUR SOUL NOW BE FILLED WITH GLADNESS Bock, Fred Bock Music Company, B-G0409	390	Traditional Swedish Melody
O LITTLE TOWN OF BETHLEHEM Shaw/Parker, Lawson-Gould, 739	178	Lewis H. Redner
O LORD MY GOD! WHEN I IN AWESOME WONDER see: HOW GREAT THOU ART	2	
O LOVE THAT WILL NOT LET ME GO Rasley, Singspiration, ZJP-7315	404	Albert L. Peace
O MASTER, LET ME WALK WITH THEE Gerig, Lillenas, AN-2339	442	H. Percy Smith
O PERFECT LOVE ———, G. Schirmer, 3837	530	Joseph Barnby
O SACRED HEAD, NOW WOUNDED Christiansen, Augsburg, 0075 Lundquist, Harold Flammer, A-5250 Smith, Hope, AG-7149, (SATB & opt instr.)	284	Hans Leo Hassler
O SAFE TO THE ROCK see: HIDING IN THEE	70	

Title	Page #	Composer
OUT IN THE HIGHWAYS AND BYWAYS OF LIFE see: MAKE ME A BLESSING	473	
OUT OF MY BONDAGE, SORROW AND NIGHT see: JESUS, I COME	401	
PASS IT ON Kaiser, Word, CS-2479	641	Kurt Kaiser
PASS ME NOT, O GENTLE SAVIOR	416	William H. Doane
PEACE I LEAVE WITH YOU Hoggard, Shawnee, A-341	64	William Wirges
PEACE, PERFECT PEACE Berglund, Beacon Hill, AN-6030	491	George T. Caldbeck
PLENTY OF ROOM IN THE FAMILY	552	William J. Gaither
PRAISE BE TO JESUS	366	William J. Gaither
PRAISE GOD, FROM WHOM ALL BLESSINGS FLOW see: ALL PEOPLE THAT ON EARTH DO DWELL Bock, "Praise God," Lorenz, S-113 Vaughan Williams, "The Old Hundredth Psalm Tune," Oxford, 42 P. 953	382, 384	Louis Bourgeois
PRAISE, MY SOUL, THE KING OF HEAVEN Andrews, G. Schirmer, 7406	339	Mark Andrews
PRAISE THE LORD, HIS GLORIES SHOW Vree, Presser, 312-40565	373	Robert Williams
PRAISE THE LORD! YE HEAVENS ADORE HIM Symonds, Fred Bock Music Company, B-G0320	335	John H. Willcox
PRAISE THE SAVIOR, YE WHO KNOW HIM	362	German Melody
PRAISE TO THE LORD, THE ALMIGHTY Gray, Pro-Art, 1856 Hanson, Hope, F 911, (SATB & brass choir opt) Sanders, Presser, 332-14827 Shaw, G. Schirmer, 10098	337	*Stralsund Gesangbuch*
PRAISE YE THE FATHER FOR HIS LOVING-KINDNESS see: PRAISE YE THE TRIUNE GOD	136	
PRAISE YE THE TRIUNE GOD Anthony, Lillenas, AN-2429 DeCou, Singspiration, ZJP-7319 Hanson, Hope, F 902, (SATB & brass choir opt)	136	Friedrich F. Flemming
PRAYER IS THE SOUL'S SINCERE DESIRE	446	William A. Schulthes
PRECIOUS LORD, TAKE MY HAND Ringwald, Shawnee, A-981	611	Thomas A. Dorsey
REACH OUT AND TOUCH Brown, Word, CS-2539	655	Charles F. Brown

Title	Page #	Composer
REDEEMED Mercer, Singspiration, ZJP-8150	646	William J. Kirkpatrick
REDEEMING LOVE Huff, Paragon, P-PM35009	199	William J. Gaither
REJOICE, THE LORD IS KING! Pfohl, Harold Flammer, A 5008 Gerig, Lillenas, AN-2220	374	John Darwall
REJOICE, YE PURE IN HEART Johnson, Singspiration, ZJP-7221	394	Arthur H. Messiter
RENEW THY CHURCH, HER MINISTRIES RESTORE	572	J. T. White's *Sacred Harp*
RESCUE THE PERISHING	661	William H. Doane
REVIVE US AGAIN Bock, "We Praise Thee, O God," Belwin-Mills, 1978 McCall, Pro-Art, 2606	574	John J. Husband
RISE UP, O MEN OF GOD Landgrave, Hope, F 920 (SATB & brass choir opt) Shaw, Lawson-Gould, 755 York, Presser, MC 239	398	William H. Walter
ROCK OF AGES, CLEFT FOR ME Olds, Schmitt, 1853 Rasley, Lorenz, C271	108	Thomas Hastings
ROOM AT THE CROSS see: THERE'S ROOM AT THE CROSS	645	
SATISFIED	100	Ralph E. Hudson
SAVIOR, AGAIN TO THY DEAR NAME WE RAISE	519	Edward J. Hopkins
SAVIOR, LIKE A SHEPHERD LEAD US Bock, Word, CS-2394 Bock, Word, CS-2407 (TTBB) Ehret, Lillenas, AN-2417 Ulrich, Manna, M-210	601	William B. Bradbury
SAVIOR, THY DYING LOVE	279	Robert Lowry
SEARCH ME, O GOD see: CLEANSE ME	425	
SECURITY	496	Unknown
SEND THE LIGHT Johnson, Singspiration, ZJP-8081	663	Charles H. Gabriel

Title	Page #	Composer
SILENT NIGHT, HOLY NIGHT	195	Franz Grüber
Berglund, Beacon Hill, AN-6047		
Curry, Presser, 312-21392		
Luboff, Walton, 2757		
Powell/Bock, "Peace, Peace," Fred Bock Music		
Company, B-G4013, (3 equal voices)		
SHACKLED BY A HEAVY BURDEN	628	
see: HE TOUCHED ME		
SIMPLY TRUSTING EVERY DAY	79	
see: TRUSTING JESUS		
SINCE I HAVE BEEN REDEEMED	644	Edwin O. Excell
SINCE JESUS CAME INTO MY HEART	639	Charles H. Gabriel
Allen, Word, CS-2521		
SING PRAISE TO GOD WHO REIGNS ABOVE	343	Bohemian Brethren's
Colber, Lillenas, AN-2425		*Kirchengesänge*
Mudde, Augsburg, 1214		
Pfautsch, Summy, 5315		
Vree, Lawson-Gould, 805		
SING THE WONDROUS LOVE OF JESUS	123	
see: WHEN WE ALL GET TO HEAVEN		
SING THEM OVER AGAIN TO ME	29	
see: WONDERFUL WORDS OF LIFE		
SITTING AT THE FEET OF JESUS	58	Asa Hull
SO SEND I YOU	664	John W. Peterson
Peterson, Singspiration, ZJP-5461		
SOFTLY AND TENDERLY	432	Will L. Thompson
SOME CHILDREN SEE HIM	181	Alfred S. Burt
Ades, Shawnee, E77		
Ehret, Shawnee, A-1414		
SOME GOLDEN DAYBREAK	312	Carl Blackmore
Boersma, Word, CS-2135		
Ferrin, Gospel Pub. House, 05 XB 0218		
SOMETHING BEAUTIFUL	656	William J. Gaither
Powell, Gaither Music, G-G5117		
SOMETHING WORTH LIVING FOR	638	William J. Gaither
____, Gaither Music, G-G5140		
SOMETIMES "ALLELUIA"	331	Chuck Girard
Gassman, Word, CS-2800		
SPEAK, LORD, IN THE STILLNESS	444	Harold Green

Title	Page #	Composer
SPIRIT, NOW LIVE IN ME Bock, Fred Bock Music Company, B-G0422	151	Bryan Jeffery Leech
SPIRIT OF GOD, DESCEND UPON MY HEART Linn, Lillenas, AT-1155	147	Frederick C. Atkinson
SPIRIT OF THE LIVING GOD	155	Daniel Iverson
STAND UP, STAND UP FOR JESUS Hadley, Pro-Art, 1358 Slauson, Singspiration, ZJP-8036 (opt Trumpet trio)	616	George J. Webb
STANDING ON THE PROMISES	69	Norman E. Johnson
STRONG, RIGHTEOUS MAN OF GALILEE	216	John Bacchus Dykes
SUN OF MY SOUL Berglund, Lillenas, AN-6023 Olds, Schmitt, 1864	62	*Katholisches Gesangbuch*
SWEET HOUR OF PRAYER Williams, Lillenas, AN-2368	439	William B. Bradbury
SWEET, SWEET SPIRIT Fettke, Manna, M-105 Kaiser, Word, CS-2499	159	Doris Akers
TAKE MY LIFE, AND LET IT BE CONSECRATED Ferrin, Lillenas, AN-1694	458	Henri A. César Malar
TAKE THE NAME OF JESUS WITH YOU	231	William H. Doane
TAKE THOU MY HAND, O FATHER	600	Friedrich Silcher
TAKE THOU OUR MINDS, DEAR LORD	467	Calvin W. Laufer
TAKE TIME TO BE HOLY	457	George C. Stebbins
TEACH ME YOUR WAY, O LORD Hawkins, Lillenas, AN-2422	472	B. Mansell Ramsey
TEACH US WHAT WE YET MAY BE see: JOYFUL, JOYFUL, WE ADORE THEE	9	Ludwig van Beethoven
TELL ME THE OLD, OLD STORY	16	William H. Doane
TELL ME THE STORIES OF JESUS	212	Frederic A. Challinor
TELL ME THE STORY OF JESUS Whitsett, Lillenas, AN-1616	215	John R. Sweney
THANK GOD FOR THE PROMISE OF SPRING _____, Gaither Music, G-G5141	110	William J. Gaither
THANKS TO GOD FOR MY REDEEMER Johnson, Singspiration, ZJP-3103	386	J. A. Hultman
THE BLOOD WILL NEVER LOSE ITS POWER Elrich, Manna, M-103	262	Andraé Crouch

Title	Page #	Composer
THE BOND OF LOVE Bock, Lillenas, AN-5050 Bock, Lillenas, AN-5046 (2 part)	544	Otis Skillings
THE CHURCH WITHIN US see: THERE'S A CHURCH WITHIN US, O LORD	551	
THE CHURCH'S ONE FOUNDATION Beck, "Upon This Rock," G. Schirmer, 11467 Rasley, Singspiration, ZJP-7256 Williams, Lillenas, AN-2331	547	Samuel S. Wesley
THE COMFORTER HAS COME	143	William J. Kirkpatrick
THE CROSS UPON WHICH JESUS DIED see: THERE'S ROOM AT THE CROSS	645	
THE EASTER SONG Herring, Word, CS-2689 Huff, Paragon. P-PM 35014	301	Anne Herring
THE FAMILY OF GOD Gaither, Gaither Music, G-G5111	543	William J. Gaither
THE FIRST NOEL Groom, Hope, A 320, (SSA or 3 unison Parts) Swift, Belwin-Mills, 1492 Vaughan Williams, "The First Nowell," Oxford, 46.509	179	English Melody
THE GOD OF ABRAHAM PRAISE! Beck, Beckenhorst, BP-1012 Kirk, Pro-Art, 1934	332	Hebrew Melody
THE GREAT PHYSICIAN	38	John H. Stockton
THE HAVEN OF REST	101	George D. Moore
THE HIDING PLACE Bolks, Manna, M-117 Elrich, Fred Bock Music Company, B-G0237	37	Bryan Jeffery Leech
THE JOY OF THE LORD	354	Alliene G. Vale
THE KING IS COMING Lane, Gaither Music, G-G5101	313	William J. Gaither
THE LIGHT OF THE WORLD IS JESUS	636	Philip P. Bliss
THE LONGER I SERVE HIM ___, Gaither Music, G-G5142	623	William J. Gaither
THE LORD BLESS YOU AND KEEP YOU Ehret, Pro-Art, 1996 Hallagan, Presser, 312-40436 Lutkin, Carl Fischer, CM-6919	522	Peter C. Lutkin

Title	Page #	Composer
THE LORD'S MY SHEPHERD, I'LL NOT WANT (BROTHER JAMES' AIR) Hustad, Hope, HA 110 Jacob, "Brother James' Air," Oxford, 43.902	42	Traditional
THE LORD'S MY SHEPHERD, I'LL NOT WANT (CRIMOND) Carmichael, Singspiration, ZJP-7238	40	Jessie S. Irvine
THE LORD'S OUR ROCK, IN HIM WE HIDE see: A SHELTER IN THE TIME OF STORM	117	
THE LORD'S PRAYER Deis, G. Schirmer, 7988	440	Albert Hay Malotte
THE LOVE OF GOD Lundberg, Lillenas, AN-2209 Skillings, Lillenas, AN-2442	18	F. M. Lehman
THE MARKETPLACE IS EMPTY see: THE KING IS COMING	313	
THE OLD RUGGED CROSS Brawn, Word, CS-2577	256	George Bennard
THE SAVIOR IS WAITING Bock, Word, CS-650 Hustad, Hope, GC-810	435	Ralph Carmichael
THE SOLID ROCK	92	William B. Bradbury
THE SPIRIT OF JESUS IS IN THIS PLACE Gaither, Gaither Music, G-G5118	157	William J. Gaither
THE STAR CAROL Ades, Shawnee, E75 Ehret, Shawnee, A 1362	201	Alfred S. Burt
THE STAR-SPANGLED BANNER Bennett, Lawson-Gould, 51722 Pfautsch, Hope, SP-681 Prussing, Gentry, G-147	688	John Stafford Smith
THE UNVEILED CHRIST Collins, Lillenas, AT-1062 Skiles, Lillenas, AN-1161, (SAB)	236	N. B. Herrell
THE VISION OF A DYING WORLD see: MACEDONIA	668	
THE WISE MAY BRING THEIR LEARNING	537	Ralph Vaughan Williams
THE WONDER OF IT ALL Shea, Chancel Music, #104	13	George Beverly Shea

Title	Page #	Composer
THERE IS A BALM OF GILEAD Brandon, Hope, A 362, (SAB) Davis, Gentry, G-234 Dawson, Kjos, T105 Ehret, Sam Fox, S126 Kirk, Pro-Art, 1527	48	Traditional Spiritual
THERE IS A FOUNTAIN FILLED WITH BLOOD	263	William Gardiner
THERE IS A GREEN HILL FAR AWAY	278	George S. Stebbins
THERE IS A NAME I LOVE TO HEAR see: O, HOW I LOVE JESUS	634	
THERE IS A PLACE OF QUIET REST see: NEAR TO THE HEART OF GOD	35	
THERE IS SUNSHINE IN MY SOUL TODAY Coates, Shawnee, A1066	630	John R. Sweney
THERE SHALL BE SHOWERS OF BLESSING	580	James McGranahan
THERE'S A CALL COMES RINGING see: SEND THE LIGHT	663	
THERE'S A CHURCH WITHIN US, O LORD Hustad, Hope, CF-105	551	Kent E. Schneider
THERE'S A QUIET UNDERSTANDING Wilson, Hope, CF 167	556	Tedd Smith
THERE'S A SWEET, SWEET SPIRIT IN THIS PLACE see: SWEET, SWEET SPIRIT	159	
THERE'S A WIDENESS IN GOD'S MERCY Fettke, Lillenas, AN-1086 Johnson, Singspiration, ZJP-7217	115	Lizzie S. Tourjée
THERE'S NOT A FRIEND LIKE THE LOWLY JESUS see: NO NOT ONE!	221	
THERE'S ROOM AT THE CROSS Stanphill, Lorenz, B174 DeCou, Singspiration, ZJP-8064	645	Ira F. Stanphill
THERE'S SOMETHING ABOUT THAT NAME Gaither, Gaither Music, G-G5106 Powell, Gaither Music, G-G5125	227	William J. Gaither
THERE'S WITHIN MY HEART A MELODY See: HE KEEPS ME SINGING	587	
THEY THAT SOW IN TEARS _____, Gaither Music, G-G5143	46	William J. Gaither
THEY THAT WAIT UPON THE LORD Rice, Hamblen Music, H-HC0009	52	Stuart Hamblen

Title	Page #	Composer
THEY'LL KNOW WE ARE CHRISTIANS BY OUR LOVE	677	Peter Scholtes
Ades, Shawnee, A 1301		
Bock, Fred Bock Music Company, B-G0133		
Bock, Fred Bock Music Company, B-G0168, (SAB)		
Bock, Fred Bock Music Company, B-G0173, (2 part)		
Wilson, Hope, AG-7101, (SAB)		
THINE IS THE GLORY	291	George Friedrich
Beck, "Easter Vigil of Mary Magdalene,"		Handel
Hinshaw, HME-209		
Handel, Lorenz, A 433		
Lee, Word, CS-2682		
THIS CHILD WE DEDICATE TO THEE	571	Henry K. Oliver
THIS COULD BE THE DAWNING OF THAT DAY	307	William J. Gaither
THIS IS MY COUNTRY	693	Al Jacobs
Ringwald, Shawnee, A 550		
Scott, Shawnee, A-1		
THIS IS MY FATHER'S WORLD	6	English Melody
Ringwald, Shawnee, A-118		
THIS IS MY SONG, O GOD OF ALL THE NATIONS	682	
see: A SONG OF PEACE		
THIS IS MY STORY, THIS IS MY SONG	67	
see: BLESSED ASSURANCE, JESUS IS MINE		
THOU DIDST LEAVE THY THRONE	170	Timothy R. Matthews
THOU, MY EVERLASTING PORTION	405	
see: CLOSE TO THEE		
THOU, WHOSE PURPOSE IS TO KINDLE	576	Rowland H. Prichard
THOU WILT KEEP HIM IN PERFECT PEACE	493	Vivian Kretz
Whitman, Lillenas, AN-2296		
THROUGH ALL THE WORLD	672	Paul F. Liljestrand
Johnson, Singspiration, ZJP-7375		
THROUGH IT ALL	43	Andraé Crouch
Elrich, Manna Music, M-22		
'TIL THE STORM PASSES BY	501	Mosie Lister
Lister, Lillenas, AL-1006		
'TIS SO SWEET TO TRUST IN JESUS	91	William J.
Bolks, Singspiration, ZJP-8151		Kirkpatrick
Rasley, Lorenz, A-413		
TO GOD BE THE GLORY	363	William H. Doane
Montgomery, Singspiration, ZJP-6021		
Pagan, Glory Sound, A 5734		
Whitman, Lillenas, AN-1144		

Title	Page #	Composer
TO GOD BE THE GLORY see: MY TRIBUTE	365	
TRUST AND OBEY Bock, Fred Bock Music Company, B-G0404	454	Daniel B. Towner
TRUSTING JESUS	79	Ira D. Sankey
TURN YOUR EYES UPON JESUS Johnson, Singspiration, ZJP-8183	621	Helen H. Lemmel
UNDER HIS WINGS Ehret, Lillenas, AN-1693	412	Ira D. Sankey
UNTIL THEN Rice, Hamblen Music, H-HC0012 Rice, Hamblen Music, H-HQ0027 (TTBB)	133	Stuart Hamblen
UP CALVARY'S MOUNTAIN see: BLESSED REDEEMER	275	
UP FROM THE GRAVE HE AROSE see: CHRIST AROSE	298	
VICTORY IN JESUS Huff, Paragon, P-PM 35015	82	Eugene M. Bartlett
WE ARE CLIMBING JACOB'S LADDER Lynn, Presser, 312-40066 Newbury, Shawnee, A-814 Wetherill, Harold Flammer, A-5802	488	Traditional Spiritual
WE ARE GOD'S PEOPLE Bock, Fred Bock Music Company, B-G0410	546	Johannes Brahms
WE ARE LIVING, WE ARE DWELLING	447	Welsh Melody
WE ARE ONE IN THE BOND OF LOVE see: THE BOND OF LOVE	544	
WE ARE ONE IN THE SPIRIT see: THEY'LL KNOW WE ARE CHRISTIANS BY OUR LOVE	677	
WE DEDICATE THIS TEMPLE Also see: THE CHURCH'S ONE FOUNDATION	568	Samuel S. Wesley
WE GATHER TOGETHER Beck, Beckenhorst, BP1047 Clough-Leighter, G. Schirmer, 306 Davis, E. C. Schirmer, 1735 Hornibrook, Shawnee, A598 Newbury, G. Schirmer, 11761 Ohl, Summy, 5318	387	Traditional Netherlands Song
WE GIVE THEE BUT THINE OWN	515	Mason and Webb's *Cantica Laudis*

Title	Page #	Composer
WE HAVE HEARD THE JOYFUL SOUND see: JESUS SAVES!	667	
WE PLOW THE FIELDS AND SCATTER THE GOOD SEED Mann, Lexicon, CS-2728	395	Johann A. P. Schulz
WE PRAISE THEE, O GOD see: REVIVE US AGAIN	574	
WE PRAISE THEE, O GOD, OUR REDEEMER See: WE GATHER TOGETHER	334	Traditional Netherlands Song
WE SING THE GREATNESS OF OUR GOD Bock, Fred Bock Music Company, B-G0120	338	*Gesangbuch der* *Herzogl,* Wirtemberg
WE THREE KINGS OF ORIENT ARE	206	John H. Hopkins, Jr.
WE'RE MARCHING TO ZION see: COME, WE THAT LOVE THE LORD	550	
WE'VE A STORY TO TELL TO THE NATIONS Leader/DeCou, Singspiration, ZJP-8014 Schubert, Lillenas, AN-1192	659	H. Ernest Nichol
WERE YOU THERE? Brandon, Hope, A 343, (SSA) DeCou, Singspiration, ZJP-3518 Gillette, Harold Flammer, A5230 Heaton, Presser, 312-40567 Ringwald, Shawnee, A32 Wagner, Lawson-Gould, 668	287	Traditional American Melody
WHAT A DAY THAT WILL BE	314	Jim Hill
WHAT A FELLOWSHIP, WHAT A JOY DIVINE See: LEANING ON THE EVERLASTING ARMS	87	
WHAT A FRIEND WE HAVE IN JESUS Coates, Harold Flammer, D-5245 (SAB) Harper, Pro-Art, 1766 Wyrtzen, Singspiration, ZJP-6033	466	Charles C. Converse
WHAT A WONDERFUL CHANGE IN MY LIFE see: SINCE JESUS CAME INTO MY HEART	639	
WHAT A WONDERFUL SAVIOR DeCou, Singspiration, ZJP-7225	372	Elisha A. Hoffman
WHAT CAN WASH AWAY MY SIN? see: NOTHING BUT THE BLOOD	266	
WHAT CHILD IS THIS, WHO, LAID TO REST? Candlyn, Carl Fischer, CM-6566 Frackenpohl, Shawnee, A4404 Hodges, Shawnee, A1224	180	Traditional English Melody

Title	Page #	Composer
Johnson, Singspiration, ZJP-3002		
Krogstad, Gospel Pub. House, 05-345		
Lowden, Harold Flammer, B5051 (SSA)		
WHAT IF IT WERE TODAY?	311	Lelia N. Morris
WHAT WONDROUS LOVE IS THIS?	283	*Southern Harmony*
Ehret, Lillenas, AN-8016		
Groom, Hope, A 323, (2-part)		
Smith, Word, CS-2676		
Wagner, Harold Flammer, A 5698		
WHEN ALL MY LABORS AND TRIALS ARE O'ER	132	
see: O, THAT WILL BE GLORY FOR ME		
WHEN HE SHALL COME	309	Almeda J. Pearce
Hustad, Hope, HA-119		
Johnson, Singspiration, ZJP-7294		
Mickelson, Lillenas, AN-1660		
WHEN I CAN READ MY TITLE CLEAR	134	Traditional American
Parker, Lawson-Gould, 51340		Melody
WHEN I SAW THE CLEANSING FOUNTAIN	359	
see: I WILL PRAISE HIM!		
WHEN I SURVEY THE WONDROUS CROSS	258	Gregorian Chant
Ehret, Lillenas, AN-2412		
Kinsman, Pro-Art, 2030		
Mallory, Crescendo 115		
WHEN MORNING GILDS THE SKIES	322	Joseph Barnby
Olds, Schmitt, 1861		
Young, G., Hope, GC-808		
WHEN PEACE, LIKE A RIVER	495	
see: IT IS WELL WITH MY SOUL		
WHEN WE ALL GET TO HEAVEN	123	Emily D. Wilson
Skillings, Lillenas, AN-1701		
WHEN WE SEE CHRIST	129	Esther Kerr Rusthoi
WHEN WE WALK WITH THE LORD	454	
see: TRUST AND OBEY		
WHERE CROSS THE CROWDED WAYS OF LIFE	665	William Gardiner's
Johnson, Augsburg, 1496		*Sacred Melodies*
WHERE HE LEADS US	607	John S. Morris
WHERE THE SPIRIT OF THE LORD IS	148	Stephen R. Adams
Bock, Fred Bock Music Company, B-G0406		
WHILE BY MY SHEEP	182	
see: HOW GREAT OUR JOY!		

Title	Page #	Composer
WHILE SHEPHERDS WATCHED THEIR FLOCKS BY NIGHT Bock, Fred Bock Music Company, B-G0200 Reynolds, Carl Fischer, CM-7712	175	George Friedrich Handel
WHITER THAN SNOW	109	William G. Fischer
WHO IS ON THE LORD'S SIDE? Peterson, Singspiration, ZJP-3202	409	C. Luise Reichardt
WHY DO I SING ABOUT JESUS? Hustad, Hope, HA 112	635	Albert A. Ketchum
WHY SHOULD HE LOVE ME SO? Collins/Bussell, Lillenas,nAT-1040	26	Robert Harkness
WONDERFUL GRACE OF JESUS Whitman, Hope, F3	114	Haldor Lillenas
WONDERFUL PEACE	494	W. G. Cooper
WONDERFUL WORDS OF LIFE	29	Philip P. Bliss
WONDROUS LOVE see: WHAT WONDROUS LOVE IS THIS?	283	
WORTHY THE LAMB	285	William J. Gaither
WOUNDED FOR ME DeCou, Singspiration, ZJP-3535 Hustad, Hope, F5	282	W. G. Ovens
YEARS I SPENT IN VANITY AND PRIDE see: AT CALVARY	415	
YESTERDAY HE DIED FOR ME see: YESTERDAY, TODAY, AND TOMORROW	76	
YESTERDAY, TODAY, AND TOMORROW Wilson, Hope, CF 138 Wyrtzen, Singspiration, ZJP-5006	76	Don Wyrtzen
YESTERDAY, TODAY, FOREVER	83	J. H. Burke
YOU SAID YOU'D COME AND SHARE ALL MY SORROWS see: FOR THOSE TEARS I DIED	436	
YOU SERVANTS OF GOD, YOUR MASTER PROCLAIM Howorth, Sam Fox, PS192 Vree, Shawnee, A-1075	360	William Croft
YOUR CAUSE BE MINE	505	A. Royce Eckhardt

Organ Selections

BASED ON HYMNTUNES FOUND IN "HYMNS FOR THE FAMILY OF GOD"

Compiled by Dr. Fred Tulan

EACH YEAR Christian composers add new hymntunes to the vast body of hymnology, and their fellow composers attempt to keep up with the resulting demand for organ embellishments of these tunes. The enclosed listing of organ selections based on hymntunes found in *Hymns for the Family of God* is by no means exhaustive. Some tunes have virtually hundreds of settings readily available (*Hyfrydol,* for example). There are some newer hymntunes (and some older ones, too) for which we were unable to locate any organ setting at this time. We have prepared space by those hymntunes so that you might add to our list as new settings are located. An effort was made to balance old and new; easy and difficult; the pleasantly naive and the pleasantly sophisticated. No attempt was made to list that inexhaustable body of hymntune materials bequeathed church organists by Johann Sebastian Bach who headed his pages of writing with *Soli Deo Gloria* (For the greater Glory of God).

ABERYSTWYTH   222
Hustad, Hymns for Organ, Hope
Peeters, Hymn Preludes for the Liturgical
   Year v.18, C.F. Peters
Thalben-Ball, 113 Variations, Novello
Vaughan Williams, Variations on —, Oxford
Willan, 30 Hymn Preludes, C.F. Peters
Wyton, Music for Lent, Harold Flammer
Young, Prelude on —, Carl Fischer

ACCLAIM
Innes, Organ Hymns for Praise and Worship, Fred Bock Music Company

ACKLEY   299

ADELAIDE   400
Goode, Improvisations, Hope
Hustad, Hymns for Organ, Hope

Lorenz, Communion Hymn Voluntaries,
   Lorenz
Purvis, 5 Folk Hymn Orisons, Word

ADESTE FIDELES   193
Demessieux, 12 Choral Preludes,
   McLaughlin & Reilly
Dethier, Variations on Christmas Carols, J.
   Fischer
Fleury, Noëls, H.W. Gray
Gigout, Modern French Organ, Oliver Ditson
Guilmant, Offertory on 2 Christmas
   Hymns, G. Schirmer
Karg-Elert, Cathedral Windows, Elkins
Lemare, Adeste Fideles, Theodore
   Presser
Piche, Rhapsody on 4 Noels, H.W. Gray
Purvis, Carol Rhapsody, Leeds

Thiman, Festal Voluntaries, Novello
Yon, Prelude Pastorale, G. Schirmer

ADORE THEE   358

ALETTA   34

ALL IS WELL   572

ALL SAINTS/NEW   668
  Lorenz, The Church Year, Lorenz
  Peeters, Hymn Preludes for the Liturgical
    Year v. 20, C.F. Peters
  Willan, 36 Short Preludes v. 3, C.F. Peters

ALL THE WAY   598
  Bock, Favorite Hymns of Faith and
    Hope, Fred Bock Music Company

ALL TO CHRIST   273

ALLELUIA   361
  Bock, He's Everything to Me, Fred Bock
    Music Company
  Bock, Alleluia, Gaither

AMAZING GRACE   107
  Bock, My God and I, Fred Bock Music
    Company
  Hustad, Hymn Sketches, Hope
  Murphee, Meditation, J. Fischer
  Purvis, 5 Folk Hymn Orisons, Word
  Ralston, Simple Gifts, Lorenz
  Shearing, Sacred Sounds, Sacred Music
    Press
  Wood, Music for Organ, Sacred Music
    Press

AMERICA   695
  Best, Prelude on —, Boston
  Coke-Jephcott, Variations and Toccata,
    H.W. Gray
  Ives, Variations, Mercury
  Peeters, 30 Short Preludes on Well Known
    Hymns, C.F. Peters
  Young, Patriotic Prelude, Harold Flammer

ANGEL'S STORY   402
  Innes, Organ Hymns for Praise and Wor-
    ship #2, Fred Bock Music Company

ANTIOCH   171
  Bock, Variations on Christmas Melodies,
    Lillenas
  Edmundson, 7 Service Preludes, J.
    Fischer
  Hustad, Hymns for Organ, Hope

Shearing, Sacred Sounds, Sacred Music
  Press
Thomas, Church Music Improvisations,
  Ethel Smith Music Corp.
Wood, Organ Book of American Folk
  Hymns, Sacred Music Press

ANY ROOM   654
  Bock, Tell the World Organ Book, Fred
    Bock Music Company

AR HYD Y NOS   4, 498
  Cronham, Before the Service, Harold
    Flammer
  Faulkes, Fantasy on Welsh Airs, Paxton
  Rogers, Contemporary Organ Settings of
    Familiar Hymns, Hope
  Wood, 7 Folk Tune Sketches, H.W. Gray

ARIEL   344
  Ashford, Hymntune Voluntaries v. 2,
    Lorenz
  Shanko, Hymntune Preludes for Organ
    #1, Broadman
  Stults, Hymn Paraphrases #1, Lorenz

ARIZONA   36

ARLINGTON   411
  Bock, Organ Sounds for Worship, Sacred
    Music Press
  Lynn, Organ Reflections, Broadman

ARMAGEDDON   409

ASH GROVE   389
  Faulkes, Fantasy on Welsh Airs, Paxton

ASSURANCE   67
  Bock, Crusade Favorites From Around the
    World, Word
  Colvin, Organ Voluntaries on Early Ameri-
    can Hymntunes, R.D. Row
  Thompson, Hymn Meditations v. 2, Lorenz

AURELIA   547, 568
  Hustad, Organ Preludes on Hymns, Hope
  Larson, Album of Hymns, Belwin-Mills
  Peeters, Hymn Preludes for the Liturgical
    Year v. 10, C.F. Peters
  Schmutz, Chorale Prelude on —, Summy

AUSTRIAN HYMN   376
  Kolher, 9 Variations, Bote & Bock
  Paine, Variations on —, Oliver Ditson
  Purvis, 7 Preludes on Tunes in American
    Hymnals, Carl Fischer

Van Hulse, Preludes on Well Known
　Hymns, J. Fischer
AWAY IN A MANGER　　　　185
　Diemer, Hymn Preludes for Meditation
　　("Mueller"), Carl Fischer
　Schmutz, 4 Hymn Preludes, Summy
　Thompson, Hymn Meditations v. 3, Lorenz
AZMON　　　　349
　Frank, 11 Standard Organ Hymns, Hope
　Juhrdahl, Festival Preludes, H.W. Gray
　Wyton, Fantasie-Improvisation, Abingdon
BALM IN GILEAD　　　　48
BARNARD　　　　516
BATTLE HYMN OF THE REPUBLIC　692
　Diggle, Fugal Fantasy on "My Eyes Have
　　Seen the Glory," G. Schirmer
　Kinder, Fantasy on —, J. Fischer
　Wilson, 21 Preludes, Lorenz
BEACH SPRING　　　　428, 507
　Colvin, Pass It On, Word
BEACON HILL　　　　470
BEECHER　　　　21
　Hustad, Hymns for Organ, Hope
　Lorenz, Gospel Hymn Voluntaries, Lorenz
　Whitford, 5 Chorale Paraphrases set 2,
　　H.W. Gray
BEL AIR　　　　535
BELLAMY　　　　320
BELMONT　　　　263
　Peeters, 30 Short Preludes on Well Known
　　Hymns, C.F. Peters
BENEDICTION　　　　522
　Altman, Organ Fantasy on —, R.D. Row
　Thompson, Hymn Meditations v. 2, Lorenz
　Walter, 6 Hymn Tune Preludes, Abingdon
　Willan, 136 Short Preludes v. 2, C.F. Peters
BENTON HARBOR　　　　372
　Figh, Hymn Tune Preludes v. 1, Broadman
BERGEN MA VIKA　　　　496
BJORKLUND MAJOR　　　　662
BLAENHAFREN　　　　447
　Penick, 3 Preludes, H.W. Gray
BLESS THE LORD　　　　379

BLESSED BE THE NAME　　　　352
　Bock, Favorite Hymns of Faith and Hope,
　　Fred Bock Music Company
　Innes, Organ Hymns for Praise and Wor-
　　ship #2, Fred Bock Music Company
BLESSED JESUS　　　　39
　Bach, A.W., Der Prakische Organist, M.
　　Bahn
　Karg-Elert, 66 Choral Improvisations v. 6,
　　E.B. Marks
BLESSED QUIETNESS　　　　145
　Innes, Organ Hymns for Praise and Wor-
　　ship #2, Fred Bock Music Company
BLOMQVIST　　　　579
BLOTT EN DAG　　　　102
　Bock, Crusade Favorites from Around the
　　World, Word
BOND OF LOVE　　　　544
BRADBURY　　　　601
　Bock, Four Hymns for the Organ ("Pleas-
　　ant Pastures"), Fred Bock Music Com-
　　pany
BREAD OF LIFE　　　　30
　Bingham, 12 Hymn Preludes set 2, H.W.
　　Gray
　Duro, 6 Contemplations, H.W. Gray
　Johnson, Deck Thyself, Augsburg
BROTHER JAMES' AIR　　　　42
　Darke, Meditations on —, Oxford
　Ellsasser, Sanctuary Organist, Word
　Wright, Prelude on —, Oxford
BRYN CALFARIA　　　　303
　Vaughan Williams, 3 Preludes on Welsh
　　Hymntunes, Stainer & Bell
BULLINGER　　　　73
　Hokanson, Organ Brevities, Hope
BUNESSAN　　　　5, 198
　Bock, He's Everything to Me, Fred Bock
　　Music Company
　Colvin, Pass It On, Word
BURDENS LIFTED　　　　60
CALLING TODAY　　　　434
　Bock, Favorite Hymns of Faith and Hope,
　　Fred Bock Music Company
CALVARY　　　　415
　Schuler, Organ Hymn-Tunes #3, Word

Darke, 3 Chorale Preludes, Novello
Innes, Organ Hymns for Praise and Worship, Fred Bock Music Company
Whitlock, 6 Hymn Preludes, Oxford

DAWNING 307
Bock, Get All Excited, Gaither

DAYBREAK 312

DENNIS 560
Manookin, Prelude on —, Avant

DEXTER 10

DIADEM 326
Hustad, Hymntune Preludes #2, Broadman

DIADEMATA 345
Hasse, Prelude on Hymntunes, Concordia
Lutkin, Transcriptions on Hymntunes, H.W. Gray
Wyton, Little Christian Year, Carl Fischer

DIVINUM MYSTERIUM 172
Bock, Organ Sounds for Worship, Sacred Music Press
Cook, Paean, Novello
Hebble, Nave, H.W. Gray
Pepping, Hymns for Organ, Bärenreiter
Purvis, Divinum Mysterium, Leeds
Thomson, Pastorale On a Christmas Plainsong, H.W. Gray

DIX 1, 202
Bingham, 36 Hymn and Carol Canons, H.W. Gray
Harris, Festal Voluntaries/Epiphany, Novello
Pritchard, Chorale Preludes set 11 #5, Cramer
Young, Organ Sounds for Service, Harold Flammer

DUKE STREET 238, 295
Gehrke, Parish Organist v. 10, Concordia
Groom, 2 Compositions, Abingdon
Thompson, Hymn Meditations v. 2, Lorenz
Whitford, 10 Preludes and Postludes, Boston

DUNBAR 453

DUNDEE 603
Best, Fantasie on —, Augener

Buck, 6 Short Chorale Preludes, Century Music Publishing Co.
Lang, 20 Hymn Tune Preludes set 1, Oxford
MacKinnon, Preludes and Offertories (Holler), H.W. Gray
Parry, 7 Chorale Preludes set 1, Novello
Ridout, 3 Preludes on Scottish Tunes, Novello

EASTER HYMN 289
Bratt, Chorale Voluntaries/Lent & Easter, World Library
Fletcher, Hymntune Voluntaries, Curwen
Lemare, Easter Morning, H.W. Gray
Young, 8 Voluntaries, Theodore Presser

EASTER SONG 301

EBENEZER (TON-Y-BOTEL) 24, 670
Maekelberge, Triptych, H.W. Gray
Noble, Fantasy on —, Schmitt, Hall & McCreary
Purvis, 7 Preludes on Tunes In American Hymnals, Carl Fischer

EIN' FESTE BURG 118
Arnell, Chorale Variation on —, Hinrichsen
Burkhard, Fantasy and Chorale on —, Bärenreiter
David, Choralwerk v. 4, Boosey & Hawkes
Dupre, 79 Chorales, H.W. Gray
Hilty, Pedal Study on —, H.W. Gray
Hustad, Hymn Sketches, Hope
Johnson, Choral Prelude on —, H.W. Gray
Karg-Elert, Chorale Improvisations v. 5, E.B. Marks
Middleschulte, Toccata on —, Leuckart
Pachelbel, Chorale Preludes, Boosey & Hawkes
Walcha, Chorale Preludes v. 1, C.F. Peters

EL NATHAN 631

ELFAKER 419

ELIZABETH 627

ELLACOMBE 248, 338
Innes, Organ Hymns For Praise and Worship #2, Fred Bock Music Company
Kreckel, Melodia Sacra, J. Fischer
Peeters, Hymn Preludes for the Liturgical Year v. 20, C.F. Peters

Whitford, 10 Chorale Paraphrases, J.
Fischer

ELLERS   519
Walters, Hymn Tune Preludes, Abingdon
Willan, 36 Short Preludes, C.F. Peters

ELLESDIE   330

ELLSWORTH   637
Bock, More Gospel Songs for All Organs,
Word

ERIE   466
Bock, He's Everything to Me, Fred Bock
Music Company
Felton, Chancel Echoes, Theodore
Presser

ERMUNTRE DICH   207
Merkel, Merkel Anthologie, Concordia
Pasquet, Chorales of Our Heritage,
Augsburg

ES IST EIN ROS'   174
Ahrens, Das Heilige Jahr, Mueller
Brahms, Chorale Preludes, Op. 122, many
editions
Diemer, 10 Hymn Preludes, Carl Fischer
Langstroth, 4 Chorale Preludes, H.W. Gray
Micheelsen, Organisten, Huellenhagen
Pasquet, Lo How A Rose, H.W. Gray
Peeters, Hymn Preludes for the Liturgical
Year v. 1, C.F. Peters
Young, Christmas Prelude on —,
Abingdon

ETERNAL LIFE   474

EVANGEL   16

EVENTIDE   500
Bingham, 36 Hymn and Carol Canons,
H.W. Gray
Kinder, Twilight Musings, Theodore Pres-
ser
Lang, 20 Hymntune Preludes set 1, Oxford
Parry, 7 Chorale Preludes set 2, Novello
Vaughan, Williams, 2 Hymntune Preludes,
Oxford
Willan, 30 Hymn Preludes v. 3, C.F. Peters

EVERLASTING LOVE   590

EWHURST   94

FABEN   335

FACE TO FACE   128
Bock, Favorite Hymns of Faith and Hope,
Fred Bock Music Company

FAITH IS THE VICTORY   71

FAITHFULNESS   98
Bock, Crusade Favorites From Around the
World, Word

FAMILY OF GOD   543
Bock, The King Is Coming, Benson

FEDERAL STREET   571
Bingham, 36 Hymn and Carol Canons,
H.W. Gray
Buck, Organ Album Modern Repertoire,
Schuberth
Whitford, 10 Chorale Paraphrases, Harold
Flammer

FESTAL SONG   398
Bingham, 12 Hymnpreludes, H.W. Gray

FILL ME NOW   153

FILL MY CUP   481
Colvin, Fill My Cup, Lord, Word

FINLANDIA   77
Allee, Your Favorite Hymns, Lillenas

FISCHER   109

FLEMMING   136

FOR ME   282

FOREST GREEN   537
Diemer, 10 Hymn Preludes, Carl Fischer
Purvis, 7 Chorale Preludes, Carl Fischer
Williams, 3 Hymn Tunes From British Isles,
Harold Flammer

FOUNDATION   32
Colvin, Organ Voluntaries, R.D. Row
Hamill, Chorale Prelude on —, H.W. Gray
Herbeck, Prelude on Well Known Hymns v.
3, Broadman
Hustad, Hymns for Organ, Hope

FRIEND   220
Felton, Chancel Echoes, Theodore
Presser
Thompson, Church Preludes, Lorenz
Young, 8 Organ Preludes, Abingdon

FRIEND OF SINNERS   219

Dupre, 79 Chorales, H.W. Gray

Edmundson, From the Western Church, H.W. Gray

Liszt, "The Christmas Tree", arr. Biggs, H.W. Gray

Ludlow, 30 Preludes, Harold Flammer

Peeters, 10 Chorale Preludes, C.F. Peters

Rowley, 4 Seasonal Improvisations, Hinrichsen

Sowerby, Advent to Whitsuntide v. 4, Hinrichsen

Young, Noël Joyeux, Harold Flammer

INTERCESSION 676

IS MY NAME 125

IT IS NO SECRET 581

ITALIAN HYMN 341, 686

Hustad, Organ Preludes on Hymns Old and New ("Giardini"), Hope

Whitford, 10 Preludes and Postludes ("Giardini"), Boston

McKinley, 10 Hymn Preludes ("Moscow"), H. W. Gray

JACOB'S LADDER 488

Hancock, Organ Book of Spirituals, Lorenz

JESU, MEINE FREUDE 277

Barlow, Variations on the Hymn of the Week pt. 2, Concordia

Diemer, 7 Hymn Preludes, Harold Flammer

Dupré, 79 Chorales, H. W. Gray

Johns, California Organist #1, Avant

Karg-Elert, 66 Chorale Preludes v. 4, E. B. Marks

Pepping, 25 Orgelchoraele, Schott

Read, Meditation on —, H. W. Gray

Stout, 8 Organ Chorales, American Composer's Alliance

JESU, MEINE ZUVERSICHT 288

Dupré, 79 Chorales, H. W. Gray

Karg-Elert, Chorale Improvisations v. 3, E. B. Marks

Schumacher, 20 Chorale Preludes, Concordia

Stout, 8 Organ Chorale Preludes, American Composer's Alliance

JESUS, I COME 401

Bock, Favorite Hymns Of Faith & Hope, Fred Bock Music Company

JESUS LOVES ME 226

Bingham, 36 Hymn and Carol Canons, H. W. Gray

JESUS NEVER FAILS 651

JESUS SAVES 667

JESUS WILL WALK WITH ME 609

JUDAS MACCABAEUS 291

Weidenhagen, Paraphrases on "Seht er kommt" (Judas), Steingraeber

JUNGST 182

KETCHUM 635

KING IS COMING 313

Bock, The King Is Coming, Benson

KING OF KINGS 242

Bock, Alleluia, Gaither

KINGS OF ORIENT 206

Bock, Organ Sounds for Worship, Sacred Music Press

KING'S WESTON 351

KINGSFOLD 208

KIRKEN 555

KREMSER 334, 387

Held, Hymn Preludes for Autumn Festivals, Concordia

Peeters, Hymn Preludes for the Liturgical Year v. 22, C. F. Peters

Willan, Parish Organist v. 2, Concordia

LANCASHIRE 595

Elmore, Mixture IV, Harold Flammer

Gehring, 6 Hymntune Preludes, Concordia

McKay, Suite on Easter Themes, J. Fischer

LASST UNS ERFREUEN 347

Bratt, Chorale Voluntaries v. 3, World Library Publications

Gaul, Easter Morn, J. Fischer

Gore, Canonic Toccata, H. W. Gray

Hustad, Hymns for the Organ, Hope

James, Toccata on — (First Sonata), H. W. Gray

Staley, Sound of the Organ, Harold Flammer

Young, Postlude ("Collage"), Harold Flammer

LAUDA ANIMA   339
Hustad, Lauda Anima, Hope
Innes, Organ Hymns for Praise and Wor-
ship, Fred Bock Music Company
Walter, 6 Hymn Tune Preludes, Abingdon

LAUDES DOMINI   322
Feibel, Variations on "When Morning",
Boston
Kingsbury, "When Morning", H. W. Gray
Lutkin, Transcriptions on Hymntunes, H.
W. Gray

LEAD ME TO CALVARY   407
Bock, 4 Hymns for the Organ, Fred Bock
Music Company

LEMMEL   621

LEONI   332
Bingham, Toccata on —, J. Fischer
Long, 3 Chorale Preludes, Oxford
Noble, Fantasy on —, Galaxy
Proulx, Prelude on —, Augsburg

LET US BREAK BREAD   564
Brandon, Variations on 2 Spirituals, Brodt
Ralston, Simple Gifts, Lorenz
Warner, 5 Spirituals, Harold Flammer

LET'S JUST PRAISE THE LORD   317
Bock, Alleluia, Gaither

LIGHT OF THE WORLD   636
Swanson, 7 Hymn Preludes, H. W. Gray

LIKE A LAMB   61

LISTER   501

LITTLE IS MUCH   512

LIVING   462

LIVING GOD   155
Bock, Favorite Hymns of Faith & Hope,
Fred Bock Music Company

LLANFAIR   297, 373
McKay, Suite on Easter Hymns, J. Fischer
Schroeder, Parish Organist v. 8, Concor-
dia
Thiman, Postlude on — (Six Pieces), G.
Schirmer

LOBE DEN HERREN   337
Karg-Elert, 66 Chorale Improvisations v. 6,
E. B. Marks

Manz, 10 Chorale Improvisations set 2,
Concordia
Shaw, Processional (Wood), Sacred
Music Press
Walcha, 20 Chorale Preludes, C. F. Peters
Young, 5 Toccatas, Harold Flammer

LOIS   151

LONDONDERRY AIR   210
Coke-Jephcott, Londonderry Air, H. W.
Gray
Hebble, Londonderry Air ("Ted Alan Worth
In Concert"), Sacred Music Press
Stanford, Intermezzo, Novello

LONESOME VALLEY   217
Jackson, Lonesome Valley ("Bristol Collection, v. 2"), Harold Flammer

LONGSTAFF   457
Schuler, Organ Encores #1, Lillenas

LORD JESUS, COME   429
Bock, He Touched Me, Gaither

LORD OF ALL   235

LORD, WE PRAISE YOU   367

LOVE   224

LOVE ME   26

LOVE OF GOD   18
Bock, The Love Of God, Lillenas

LUX PRIMA   293

LYONS   336
Bielawa, in "Consoliere" v. 1, #3, World
Library Publications
Johnson, Parish Organist v. 11, Concordia
Lorenz, 21 Preludes on Standard Hymns,
Lorenz

MADRID   342
Bunjes, Parish Organist v. 3, ("Spanish
Hymn"), Concordia

MAITLAND   504

MALOTTE   440
Stickles, G. Schirmer

MAORI   425

MARANATHA   414

MARCHING TO ZION   550
Wyton, Preludes for Christian Praise, Sacred Music Press

MARGARET 170
Bock, Variations On Christmas Melodies, Lillenas

MARION 394
Peeters, Hymntune Preludes for Liturgical Year v. 6, C. F. Peters
Sowerby, 2 Chorale Preludes, H. W. Gray
Young, 6 Pieces, Word

MARTYRDOM 274
Jewell, Practical Service Music, Carl Fischer
Powell, Parish Organist v. 11, Concordia
Young, Easy Organ Pieces, Harold Flammer

MARYTON 442, 559

MATERNA 690
Demarest, Chorale Prelude on —, G. Schirmer
Hokanson, Organ Brevities, Hope
Purvis, 5 Folk Hymn Orisons, Word

MC AFEE 35
Innes, Organ Hymns for Praise and Worship #2, Fred Bock Music Company

MC CABE 663

MC CONNELSVILLE 433

MC DANIEL 639

MELITA 216, 679
Calver, Fantasy on Favorite Hymntunes, Schmidt
Gaul, Hymn of the American Navy, H. W. Gray
Innes, Organ Hymns for Praise and Worship #2, Fred Bock Music Company
Vergolet, Storm Fantasy, Paxton

MENDEBRAS 12
Ashford, Hymntune Voluntaries v. 2, Lorenz

MENDELSSOHN 184
Gehrke, Parish Organist v. 2, Concordia
Lutkin, Transcriptions on Hymntunes, H. W. Gray
Purvis, Carol Rhapsody, MCA
Wyton, Prelude Fanfare and March, Harold Flammer

MERCY 162
Gottschalk, Everybody's Favorite Series #37, AMSCO
Hustad, Hymns for Organ, Hope
Thompson, Hymn Meditations v. 3, Lorenz
Walton, Fantasy on—, Boston
Young, Chorale Preludes on 7 Hymntunes, Harold Flammer

MESSAGE 659

MIEIR 230
Bock, His Name Is Wonderful, Vol 2, Manna

MILES LANE 327
Hustad, Hymn Tune Preludes v. 2, Broadman
McKay, Suite on Easter Themes, J. Fischer
Webber, Prelude on —, Cramer
Whitney, Improvisation on —, H. W. Gray

MILLS 164

MINERVA 629

MIT FREUDEN ZART 343
Distler, Kurze Choralbearbeitungen, Bärenriter
Pepping, Grosses Orgelbuch v. 3, Schott
Walcha, Chorale Preludes v. 2, C. F. Peters

MONTROSE 626
Bock, My God And I, Fred Bock Music Company

MOODY 105

MORE LOVE TO THEE 476
Andrews, Changes on 3 Hymntunes, J. Fischer
Thompson, Hymn Melodies v. 1, Lorenz
Wilson, Gospel Hymn Voluntaries, Lorenz

MORECAMBE 147
Couper, Ancient Melodies and Hymns, Harold Flammer
Elmore, Mixture IV, Harold Flammer
Hustad, Organ Preludes on Hymns Old and New, Hope
Jewell, Practical Service Music, C. Fischer
Young, Hymntune Meditations v. 3, Lorenz

MORRIS 485

MOUNT CALVARY 270
Bock, Alleluia, Gaither

MY COUNTRY   693
Bock, Organ Music for Ceremonial Occasions, Shawnee Press

MY REDEEMER   228

MY SAVIOR'S LOVE   223
Bock, Favorite Hymns of Faith & Hope, Fred Bock Music Company

MY TRIBUTE   365

NATIONAL ANTHEM   688
Statham, Lament, Novello (as improvised moments after the assassination of President Kennedy)

NATIONAL HYMN   687
Bingham, 36 Hymn and Carol Canons, H. W. Gray
Nordman, Thanksgiving Melody, Hansen
Peeters, Hymn Preludes for the Liturgical Year v. 23, C. F. Peters

NEAR THE CROSS   254
Nolte, Gospel Hymn Voluntaries, Lorenz

NEED   443
Bock, More Gospel Songs for All Organs, Word
Larsen, Album of Familiar Hymns, Belwin-Mills
Van Hulse, 10 Preludes on Well Known Hymns, J. Fischer

NETTLETON   318, 513
Ashford, Hymntune Voluntaries v. 2, Lorenz
Hancock, Bristol Collection, Flammer
Thompson, Hymntune Meditations v. 3, Lorenz

NEUMARK   605
Diemer, 10 Hymnpreludes for Prayer and Praise, C. Fischer
McKinney, Bristol Collection #1, Harold Flammer

NEVER OUTLOVE   452
Bock, Get All Excited, Gaither

NICAEA   323
Canning, Parish Organist v. 2, Concordia
Goemanne, One Faith In Song, World Library Publications

Post, Fantasy on Holy, Holy, Holy, Ars Nova
Rohlig, 30 Settings of Familiar Hymntunes, Abingdon

NO, NOT ONE   221

NO OTHER PLEA   75

NORRIS   607
Bock, Tell the World Organ Book, Fred Bock Music Company

NUN DANKET   525
Asma, Fantasie on —, Alsbach
Bender, 30 Little Chorale Preludes, Bärenreiter
Bristol, Bristol Collection #2, Harold Flammer
Dupré, 79 Chorales, H. W. Gray
Hustad, Hymn Sketches, Hope
Jackson, Festal Voluntaries, Novello
Liszt, Nun Danket, Boosey & Hawkes
Quesnel, 5 Variations on —, Gentry Publications
Telemann, Organ Works bk. 1, Bärenreiter

NYACK   83

O, HOW I LOVE JESUS   634
Innes, Organ Hymns for Praise and Worship, Fred Bock Music Company

O PERFECT LOVE   530
Hustad, Hymn Sketches, Hope
Schreiner, Organ Voluntaries v. 2, J. Fischer
Titcomb, Wedding Day, Harold Flammer

O STORE GUD   2
Bock, How Great Thou Art, Word
Lorenz, Prelude on —, Abingdon
Shaffer, Hymntune Meditations, Broadman

OLD 100TH   381, 382, 384
Bock, Organ Sounds for Worship, Sacred Music Press
Bristol, Bristol Collection #1, Harold Flammer
Hamburger, 50 Koralbearbejdelelsen, Hansen (England)
Joubert, Prelude on —, Oxford
Truette, 5 Chorale Preludes, Schmidt
Wesley, Selection of Psalm Tunes, Novello
Willan, 30 Hymnpreludes, C. F. Peters

Descants and Free Accompaniments

The sensitive church organist will *lead* singing with the *words* being highlighted through creative registration, modulations, and the use of mid-hymn or last-verse harmonizations, free accompaniments and/or descants by the choir or by the congregation. The goal is surely the enhancement of the poetry of the text. Best bets among the many fine accompaniment aids for the organist are listed below:

A Book Of Descants, Alan Gray (less known, but a favorite of church music specialist Leo Sowerby in earlier days) Oxford University Press.

Descant Hymn Tune Book, Geoffrey Shaw, (in two volumes, only the "complete edition" has the organ part included) Oxford University Press.

50 Free Organ Accompaniments to Well-known Hymn Tunes, T. Tertius Noble, and the companion volume, *Free Organ Accompaniments to 100 Well-known Hymn Tunes*, (more difficult) Belwin-Mills Music Corp.

Free Organ Accompaniments to Festival Hymns, many contributors including: David Johnson, Jan Bender, Ronald Nelson, Daniel Moe, Robert Wetzler. Augsburg Publishing House.

New Settings of 21 Well-known Hymn Tunes, Dale Wood, (instrumental or vocal descants), Augsburg Publishing House.

Variants on Hymntunes for Congregational Singing, Fred Bock, (rich modulations and harmonic structures of today), Fred Bock Music Company.

See also the listing of Last-verse Harmonizations and Descants on page 219.

V

Indexes

Alphabetical Index of First-lines of Every Verse of Every Hymn

Alphabetical Listing of Hymntunes with Metric Division

Italicized hymntunes have last-verse harmonizations and/or descants.

Metrical Index of Hymntunes

Quebec, 451
Tallis' Canon, 518
Truro, 239
Tryggare Kan Ingen Vara, 89
Woodworth, 417

L.M. with Refrain
Happy Day, 647
He Leadeth Me, 606
Higher Ground, 469
Solid Rock, 92
Sweney, 477

L.M.D.
Sweet Hour, 439

3.3.7.5.
Bless the Lord, 379

4.4.4.4.
Lord, We Praise You, 367

4.4.4.5.15.4.4.
Holy, Holy, 149

4.4.7.4.4.7.4.4.4.4.7.
W. Zlobie Lezy, 194

4.5.7.D. with Refrain
Dexter, 10

5.3.6.5.5.6. with Refrain
Lord of All, 235

5.4.5.4. D.
Adelaide, 400
Daybreak, 312

5.4.5.4.6.6.5.4.
Almost, 437

5.5.5.4.D.
Bunessan, 5, 198

5.5.5.4.D. with Refrain
Christlike, 480

5.5.6.5.6.5.6.5. with Refrain
Judas Maccabeus, 291

5.6.8.5.5.8.
Crusaders' Hymn, 240

6.4.6.4. with Refrain
Need, 443

6.4.6.4.D.
Bread of Life, 30
Hall, 467

6.4.6.4.6.6.6.4.
Camacha, 472
Something For Jesus, 279

6.5.6.4. with Refrain
Christ Arose, 298

6.5.6.5.
Quietude, 444

6.5.6.5.D.
Bjorklund Major, 662
King's Weston, 351
Longstaff, 457
Penitence, 122

6.5.6.5.D. with Refrain
St. Gertrude, 617
Wye Valley, 497

6.5.6.5.6.5.D.
Armegeddon, 409

6.6.4.
Maranatha, 414

6.6.4.6.6.6.4.
America, 695
Italian Hymn, 341, 686
Olivet, 84

6.6.5.6.6.5.7.8.6.
Jesu, Meine Freude, 277

6.6.6.4.
For Me, 282

6.6.6.5.6.6.6.5.D.
Ash Grove, 389

10.10.10.13. with Refrain
I Need Jesus, 450

10.10.10.15.
I Know A Fount, 265

10.10.11.11.
Hanover, 360
Lyons, 336

11.6.11.6. with Refrain
McCabe, 663

11.7.11.7. with Refrain
Carmichael, 435
Thompson, 432

11.8.11.8. with Refrain
Blessed Jesus, 39
God Leads Us, 597
Good Ship, 101
He Hideth My Soul, 120
Light of the World, 636

11.8.11.9. with Refrain
Ville Du Havre, 495

11.9.11.9. with Refrain
Washed In the Blood, 259

11.9.12.8. with Refrain
Calvary Covers It, 250

11.10.10.11. with Refrain
Only Believe, 585

11.10.11.8. with Refrain
Praise To Jesus, 366

11.10.11.10.
Bergen Ma Vika, 496
Carla, 81
O Perfect Love, 530
Pearce, 309
So Send I You, 664

11.10.11.10. with Refrain
Faithfulness, 98
Go Ye, 674
Jesus Will Walk With Me, 609

O Store Gud, 2
One Day, 22
Tidings, 658
Until Then, 133

11.10.11.10.11.10.
Finlandia, 538, 682

11.10.11.10.11.10.11.12.
Londonderry Air, 210

11.11. with Refrain
Revive Us Again, 574

11.11.3.8.9.
Symphony, 546

11.11.11.5.
Flemming, 136

11.11.11.9.
Turlock, 69

11.11.11.10. with Refrain
Hingham, 412
I'd Rather Have Jesus, 650

11.11.11.11.
Away In A Manger, 185
Cradle Song, 187
Foundation, 456
Gordon, 456
St. Denio, 319

11.11.11.11. with Refrain
Fischer, 109
Security, 594
To God Be the Glory, 363

11.11.12.11. with Refrain
Intercession, 676

11.12.12.10.
Nicaea, 323

12.8.12.8. with Refrain
McDaniel, 639

12.9.12.9.
Precious Lord, 611

Topical Index of Hymntunes

(Expanded)

COMMUNION (See also Jesus Christ
—Atonement, Crucifixion and Death)

A hymn of joy we sing	565
Beneath the cross	253
Blest be the tie that binds	560
Calvary covers it all	250
Come to Calvary's	276
Here, O my Lord	567
In the cross	251
Jesus, Thy blood	268
Let all mortal flesh	166
Let us break bread	564
O sacred Head	284
When I survey	258

CONCERN FOR OTHERS

Eternal Father	679
For you I am praying	676
I am praying for you	676
I have a Savior	676
Reach out and touch	655
The Savior is waiting	435
They'll know we are Christians	677
We are one in the spirit	677

CONFESSION AND REPENTANCE

At Calvary	415
Cleanse me	425
Come, ye sinners	428
Dear Lord and Father	422
I lay my sins	427
Just as I am	417
Kind and merciful God	419
Lord, I want to be	421
Pass me not	416
Search me, O God	425
Years I spent in vanity	415

CONFIRMATION (See Baptism and
Dedication; See also Dedication
Services-Children)

CONFLICT (See Loyalty and
Courage)

DEDICATION AND DEVOTION

All for Jesus	459
Draw me nearer	455
I am Thine, O Lord	455
I could never outlove	452
I need Jesus	450
I'll live for Him	453
Jesus, the very thought	465
Jesus, Thou joy	451
Jesus, we just want to thank You	461
Living for Jesus	462
My Jesus, I love Thee	456
My wonderful Lord	368
Savior, Thy dying love	279
Take my life	458
Take Thou our minds	467
Take time to be holy	457
Trust and obey	454
We are living	447
What a friend	466
When we walk	454

DEATH (See Funeral Hymns)

DEDICATION SERVICES
Church Building

God whose giving	513
The Church's one foundation	547
We dedicate this temple	568

**Children (See also Baptism and
    Dedication)**

Children of the heavenly Father	89
I think when I read	213
Jesus loves me!	226
This child we dedicate	571

Organ

All creatures of our God (*vs. 5*)	347
God whose giving	513

Ordination

Blest be the tie	560
Brethren, we have met	321
God is at work within you	584
God, whose giving	513
Have Thine own way	400
Take my life	458

Scriptural Allusions In Hymns

By John Seider

OLD TESTAMENT	

GENESIS	
1	338
1:1	4
:3	12
3:8-9	18
:17-18	171
8:22	98, 110, 395
9:13-15	404
24:27	332
28:12	488
32:10	26

EXODUS	
3:14	283, 332
13:21	376, 389, 608
15:23	585
16:7	5
17:6	598
32:26	409
33:11	455
:22	120
34:22	392

LEVITICUS	
19:18	655
25:10	695
26:12	657

NUMBERS	
6:24-26	522
9:16	376, 389, 608
20:11	598
21:9	621

DEUTERONOMY	
1:33	376, 389, 608
6:5	398, 467, 572
8:16	376
26:8	7
31:6, 8	336
32:3	325, 326, 327, 360
:10	545
32:47	687
33:25	98, 102, 112, 120, 366
:27	87, 523

JOSHUA	
1:5	336
:9	32, 528
23:14	69
24:15	540

RUTH	
2:12	222, 337, 412, 459, 523, 587

I SAMUEL	
2:1, 26	571
3:10	444
7:12	318

II SAMUEL	
7:22	104, 323, 416
22:2	118, 614
:11-12	336, 632

I KINGS	
18:41	580
19:11-12	422, 502, 572

II KINGS	
2:8	523

I CHRONICLES	
16:10	644

:8	92, 260, 268, 344, 567
:11	430
:12	345
:16	81, 231, 235, 242, 652
20:4, 6	288, 298, 664
:15	125
21:2	133, 390, 546, 547
:4	77, 84, 96, 128, 129, 134, 314
:6	21, 172
:9	311, 390, 546, 547
:21	82, 123
:23	131, 636
:27	125

22:4	128, 223, 282, 307, 313, 314, 344, 625
:5	131, 288, 298, 317, 557, 636, 664
:6	477
:7	303, 304, 305, 306, 307, 309, 310, 311, 312, 313, 315
:13	21, 172
:14	72, 123, 405, 639
:17	227
:20	303, 304, 305, 306, 307, 309, 310, 311, 312, 313, 392, 429, 495

Alphabetical Index of Last-verse Harmonizations and Descants

(By Title and Hymntune)

COME, THOU ALMIGHTY KING   341, 686   ITALIAN HYMN
last verse organ harmonization by Van Denman Thompson and Fred Bock (G)

COME, THOU FOUNT OF EVERY BLESSING   318   NETTLETON
last verse organ harmonization by Richard Bolks (D mod to Eb)

COME, THOU LONG-EXPECTED JESUS   168   HYFRYDOL
last verse soprano descant by Paul Sjolund (F)

COME, YE THANKFUL PEOPLE, COME   392   ST. GEORGE'S WINDSOR
last verse organ harmonization by John Ness Beck (F)

CROWN HIM WITH MANY CROWNS   345   DIADEMATA
last verse soprano descant by Paul Sjolund (D)

FAITH OF OUR FATHERS   526   ST. CATHERINE
last verse soprano descant by Bob Burroughs (G)

GLORIOUS THINGS OF THEE ARE SPOKEN   376   AUSTRIAN HYMN
last verse organ harmonization by Gordon Young (F)

GOD OF GRACE AND GOD OF GLORY   528   CWM RHONDDA
last verse organ harmonization by Robert Elmore (G)

GOD OF OUR FATHERS   687   NATIONAL HYMN
last verse organ harmonization by Fred Bock (Eb mod to F)

GOD THE OMNIPOTENT   353   RUSSIAN HYMN
last verse soprano descant by Paul Sjolund (D)

HARK! THE HERALD ANGELS SING   184   MENDELSSOHN
last verse soprano descant by Paul Liljestrand (F)

HE LEADETH ME, O BLESSED THOUGHT   626   HE LEADETH ME
last verse soprano descant by Tom Fettke (D)

HOLY! HOLY! HOLY! LORD GOD ALMIGHTY   323   NICAEA
last verse soprano descant by David McK. Williams (D)

I LOVE YOUR KINGDOM, LORD   545   ST. THOMAS
Handbell descant by Darlene Lawrence (F)

IMMORTAL, INVISIBLE, GOD ONLY WISE   319   ST. DENIO
last verse organ harmonization by Mary E. Caldwell (Ab)

JESUS SHALL REIGN WHERE'ER THE SUN   238   DUKE STREET
last verse organ harmonization by Steven R. Quesnel (Db mod to D)

LEAD ON, O KING ETERNAL   595   LANCASHIRE
last verse soprano descant by John Ness Beck (C)
last verse organ harmonization by John Ness Beck (C)

THE SOLID ROCK   92   SOLID ROCK
    last verse organ harmonization by Ronn Huff (G)

THIS IS MY FATHER'S WORLD   6   TERRA BEATA
    last verse organ harmonization by Richard Purvis (Eb)

WE GATHER TOGETHER   387   KREMSER
    last verse soprano descant by Tom Fettke (D)

WHEN MORNING GILDS THE SKIES   322   LAUDES DOMINI
    last verse organ harmonization by Fred Bock (C)

ORGAN HARMONIZATIONS

ALL CREATURES OF OUR GOD AND KING   347   LASST UNS ERFREUEN
last verse organ harmonization by Fred Bock (Eb mod to F)

ALL GLORY, LAUD AND HONOR   249   ST. THEODULPH
last verse organ harmonization by A. Royce Eckhardt (Bb)
last verse soprano descant by A. Royce Eckhardt (Bb)

ALL HAIL THE POWER OF JESUS' NAME   325   CORONATION
last verse organ harmonization by Fred Bock (G)

ANGELS FROM THE REALMS OF GLORY   190   REGENT SQUARE
last verse organ harmonization by Fred Bock (Bb)

BECAUSE HE LIVES   292   RESURRECTION
last chorus organ harmonization by Ronn Huff (Ab mod to A)

COME, CHRISTIANS, JOIN TO SING   342   MADRID
last verse organ harmonization by Fred Bock (Ab mod to A)

COME, THOU ALMIGHTY KING   341, 686   ITALIAN HYMN
last verse organ harmonization by Van Denman Thompson and Fred Bock (G)

COME, THOU FOUNT OF EVERY BLESSING   318   NETTLETON
last verse organ harmonization by Richard Bolks (D mod to Eb)

COME, YE THANKFUL PEOPLE, COME   392   ST. GEORGE'S WINDSOR
last verse organ harmonization by John Ness Beck (F)

GLORIOUS THINGS OF THEE ARE SPOKEN   376   AUSTRIAN HYMN
last verse organ harmonization by Gordon Young (F)

GOD OF GRACE AND GOD OF GLORY   528   CWM RHONDDA
last verse organ harmonization by Robert Elmore (G)

GOD OF OUR FATHERS   687   NATIONAL HYMN
last verse organ harmonization by Fred Bock (Eb mod to F)

IMMORTAL, INVISIBLE, GOD ONLY WISE   319   ST. DENIO
last verse organ harmonization by Mary E. Caldwell (Ab)

JESUS SHALL REIGN WHERE'ER THE SUN   238   DUKE STREET
last verse organ harmonization by Steven R. Quesnel (Db mod to D)

LEAD ON, O KING ETERNAL   595   LANCASHIRE
last verse soprano descant by John Ness Beck (C)
last verse organ harmonization by John Ness Beck (C)

LOVE DIVINE, ALL LOVES EXCELLING   21   BEECHER
   last verse organ harmonization by Robert J. Powell (Bb)

O COME, O COME, EMMANUEL   169   VENI EMMANUEL
   last verse organ harmonization by Richard Purvis (G
   last verse soprano descant by Richard Purvis (G)

O WORSHIP THE KING   336   LYONS
   last verse organ harmonization by Fred Bock (Ab mod to A)

O ZION, HASTE, THY MISSION HIGH FULFILLING   658   TIDINGS
   last verse organ harmonization by Eugene Butler (Bb)

PRAISE THE LORD, YE HEAVENS ADORE HIM   335   FABEN
   last verse organ harmonization by Ovid Young (Bb)

REJOICE, YE PURE IN HEART   394   MARION
   last verse organ harmonization by Fred Bock (G)

THE CHURCH'S ONE FOUNDATION   547   AURELIA
   last verse organ harmonization by Eric Thiman (Eb)

THE FIRST NOEL   179   THE FIRST NOEL
   last verse organ harmonization by Jan Sanborn (D)
   last verse soprano descant by Jan Sanborn (D)

THE KING IS COMING   313   KING IS COMING
   last chorus organ harmonization by Ronn Huff (A mod to Bb)

THE SOLID ROCK   92   SOLID ROCK
   last verse organ harmonization by Ronn Huff (G)

THIS IS MY FATHER'S WORLD   6   TERRA BEATA
   last verse organ harmonization by Richard Purvis (Eb)

WHEN MORNING GILDS THE SKIES   322   LAUDES DOMINI
   last verse organ harmonization by Fred Bock (C)

Additional last verse harmonizations for organ may be found at the end of the chapter, "Organ selections based on Hymntunes found in *Hymns for the Family of God*," page 153.

SOPRANO DESCANTS

A MIGHTY FORTRESS IS OUR GOD   118   EIN' FESTE BURG
last verse soprano descant by Mary E. Caldwell (C)

ALL CREATURES OF OUR GOD AND KING   347   LASST UNS ERFREUEN
last verse soprano descant by Fred Bock (Eb mod to F)

ALL GLORY, LAUD AND HONOR   249   ST. THEODULPH
last verse organ harmonization by A. Royce Eckhardt (Bb)
last verse soprano descant by A. Royce Eckhardt (Bb)

AMERICA, THE BEAUTIFUL   690   MATERNA
first and last verse soprano descants by Fred Bock (Bb)

BATTLE HYMN OF THE REPUBLIC   692   BATTLE HYMN OF THE REPUBLIC
refrain descant for sopranos by Fred Bock (Bb)

CHRIST THE LORD IS RISEN TODAY   289   EASTER HYMN
first and fourth verse trumpet I descant by Paul Sjolund (C concert)
second and fourth verse trumpet II descant by Paul Sjolund (C concert)
third and fourth verse soprano descant by Paul Sjolund (C)

COME, THOU LONG-EXPECTED JESUS   168   HYFRYDOL
last verse soprano descant by Paul Sjolund (F)

CROWN HIM WITH MANY CROWNS   345   DIADEMATA
last verse soprano descant by Paul Sjolund (D)

FAITH OF OUR FATHERS   526   ST. CATHERINE
last verse soprano descant by Bob Burroughs (G)

GOD THE OMNIPOTENT   353   RUSSIAN HYMN
last verse soprano descant by Paul Sjolund (D)

HARK! THE HERALD ANGELS SING   184   MENDELSSOHN
last verse soprano descant by Paul Liljestrand (F)

HE LEADETH ME, O BLESSED THOUGHT   626   HE LEADETH ME
last verse soprano descant by Tom Fettke (D)

HOLY! HOLY! HOLY! LORD GOD ALMIGHTY   323   NICAEA
last verse soprano descant by David McK. Williams (D)

LEAD ON, O KING ETERNAL   595   LANCASHIRE
last verse soprano descant by John Ness Beck (C)
last verse organ harmonization by John Ness Beck (C)

LET ALL THINGS NOW LIVING   389   ASH GROVE
last verse soprano descant by Katherine K. Davis (F)

MY COUNTRY, 'TIS OF THEE   695   AMERICA
last verse soprano descant by Mary E. Caldwell (F)

O COME, ALL YE FAITHFUL   193   ADESTE FIDELES
soprano chorus descant by Fred Bock (Ab)

O COME, O COME, EMMANUEL   169   VENI EMMANUEL
last verse organ harmonization by Richard Purvis (G)
last verse soprano descant by Richard Purvis (G)

O FOR A THOUSAND TONGUES TO SING   349   AZMON
last verse soprano descant by Eugene Butler (Ab)

O, HOW I LOVE JESUS   634   O HOW I LOVE JESUS
chorus soprano descant by Ralph H. Goodpasteur (G)

THE FIRST NOEL   179   THE FIRST NOEL
last verse organ harmonization by Jan Sanborn (D)
last verse soprano descant by Jan Sanborn (D)

WE GATHER TOGETHER   387   KREMSER
last verse soprano descant by Tom Fettke (D)

HANDBELL DESCANTS

I LOVE YOUR KINGDOM, LORD   545   ST. THOMAS
    handbell descant by Darlene Lawrence (F)

PRAISE, MY SOUL, THE KING OF HEAVEN   339   LAUDA ANIMA
    last verse two-octave handbell descant by Bob Burroughs (D)

REJOICE, THE LORD IS KING   374   DARWALL'S 148th
    last verse two-octave handbell descant by Bob Burroughs (C)

INSTRUMENTAL DESCANTS

CHRIST THE LORD IS RISEN TODAY   289   EASTER HYMN
    first and fourth verse trumpet I descant by Paul Sjolund (C concert)
    second and fourth verse trumpet II descant by Paul Sjolund (C concert)

Alphabetical Index of
Arrangers, Authors, Composers,
Sources, and Translators

Allan R. Petker

Cowper, William (1731-1800) W: 263-603
Cox, Frances E. (1812-1897) W: 343
Coxe, Arthur C. (1818-1896) W: 447
Croft, William (1678-1727) M: 360, 370
Croly, George (1780-1860) W: 147
Crosby, Fanny J. (1820-1915) W: 67, 120, 215, 254, 363, 405, 416, 434, 455, 598, 646, 661
Crouch, Andraé (1945-   ) W/M: 43, 262, 365, 379
Crüger, Johann (1598-1662) M: 144, 277, 288, 525
Cushing, William O. (1823-1902) W: 70, 412
Cutler, Henry S. (1824-1902) M: 668

Dahlgren, James E. (1930-   ) R: 355
Darwall, John (1731-1789) M: 232, 374
Davies, Samuel (1723-1761) W: 104
Davis, Frank M. (1839-1896) M: 125
Davis, Katherine K. (1892-   ) W: 389; Arr: 389
Dearle, Edward (1806-1891) M: 567
Demarest, Gary W. (1926-   ) R: 113, 160, 511
Dix, William C. (1837-1898) W: 180, 202
Dixon, Helen C. (AKA Helen C. Alexander-Dixon) (1877-1969) W: 594
Doane, William Howard (1832-1915) M: 16, 231, 254, 363, 416, 455, 476, 661
Doddridge, Philip (1702-1751) W: 7, 647
Donne, John (1573-1631) R: 90
Dorsey, Thomas A. (1899-   ) W/M: 611
Doving, Carl (1867-1937) W: 555
Draper, William H. (1855-1933) W: 347
Dobois, Theodore (1837-1924) M: 358
Duffield, George (1818-1888) W: 616
Dunbar, C. R. (19th century) M: 453
Dungan, Olive (1903-   ) M: 474
Dwight, Timothy (1752-1817) W: 545
Dykes, John Bacchus (1823-1876) M: 51, 216, 323, 465, 540, 679

Ebeling, Johann G. (1637-1676) M: 203
Eckhardt, A. Royce (1937-   ) M: 390, 428, 505; Arr: 249, 278
Edmunds, Lidie H. (19th century) W: 75
Edwards, Robert Lansing (b. 1915) W: 513
Ellerton, John (1826-1893) W: 353, 519
Elliott, Charlotte (1789-1871) W: 417

Elliott, Emily E.S. (1836-1897) W: 170
Elliott, Ruth (1887-   ) W: 510
Ellor, James (1819-1899) M; 326
Elmore, Robert (1913-   ) Arr: 528
Elvey, George J. (1816-1893) M; 345, 392
Emurian, Ernest K. (1912-   ) W: 568
English Carol W/M: 179
English Melody M: 6, 180, 208
Evans, David (1874-1948) M: 468; Arr: 5
Excell, Edwin O. (1851-1921) W: 644; M: 107, 644
Faber, Frederick W. (1814-1863) W: 115, 526
Farjeon, Eleanor (1881-1965) W: 5
Farrington, Harry Webb (1879-1930) W: 216
Fawcett, John (1740-1817) W: 520, 560
Featherston, William Ralph (1846-1873) W: 456
Ferguson, Manie Payne (19th century) W: 145
Fettke, Tom (1941-   ) Arr: 387, 606
Fischer, William Gustavus (1835-1912) M: 109, 619
Flemming, Friedrich F. (1778-1813) M: 136
Flint, Annie Johnson (1866-1932) W: 112
Fosdick, Harry Emerson (1878-1969) W: 528
Foulkes, William Hiram (1877-1962) W: 467
Foundling Hospital Collection (1796) W: 335
Fox, Baynard L. (1932-   ) W/M: 648
Francis of Assissi (1182-1226) W: 347, 474
Francis, Samuel Trevor (1834-1925) W: 24
Franck, Johann (1618-1677) W: 277
Franz, Ignaz (1719-1790) W: 385
French Carol W: 192; M: 166, 192
Fullerton, W.Y. (1857-1932) W: 210

Gabriel, Charles Hutchinson (1856-1932) W: 132, 223, 653, 663; M: 132, 223, 450, 469, 639, 653, 663
Gaelic Melody M: 5, 198
Gaither, Gloria (1942-   ) W: 39, 46, 110, 150, 157, 199, 227, 235, 242, 270, 285, 292, 307, 313, 317, 366, 397, 429, 452, 461, 543, 548, 552, 596, 647, 656; R: 90; 200, 243, 350, 569, 570, 583, 593
Gaither, William J. (1936-   ) W: 46, 110, 135, 150, 157, 227, 235, 242, 270, 285, 292, 307, 313, 317, 397, 429, 452, 461, 543, 548, 552, 596, 623, 628, 652; M: 39, 46, 110,

Oakeley, Frederick (1802-1880) W: 193
Oatman, Johnson Jr. (1856-1922) W: 221, 469
Ogilvie, Lloyd John (1930-   ) R: 371
Ölander, Anna (1861-1939) W: 642
Oldham, Dale (1903-   ) W: 270, 638
Oliver, Henry K. (1800-1885) M: 571
Olson, Ernst W. (1870-1958) W: 89
Olsson, Karl A. (1913-   ) W: 390
Orr, J. Edwin (1912-   ) W: 425
Ortlund, Anne (1923-   ) W: 668
Ortlund, Raymond C. (1923-   ) R: 333
Osler, Edward (1798-1863) W: 335
Our Song of Hope R: 529 See Reformed Church of America
Ovens, W.G. (1870-1945) W/M: 282
Owen, William (1814-1893) M: 303
Owens, Jimmy (1930-   ) W: 149; M: 149, 575
Owens, Priscilla Jane (1829-1907) W: 667
Oxenham, John (1852-1941) W: 685

Page, Kirby (1890-1957) R: 33, 673
Palmer, Ray (1808-1887) W: 84, 451
Parker, Edwin P. (1836-1925) Arr: 162
Parker, William H. (1845-1929) W: 212
Parry, Joseph (1841-1903) M: 222
Patrick, St. (387?-465?) R: 643
Peace, Albert Lister (1844-1912) M: 404
Peale, Norman Vincent (1898-   ) R: 80
Pearce, Almeda J. (1893-   ) W/M: 309
Pearson, E. Lincoln (1917-   ) W: 496
Perronet, Edward (1726-1792) W: 325, 326, 327
Peters, Mary (1813-1856) W: 498
Peterson, John W. (1921-   ) W: 36, 219, 305, 626, 657; M: 36, 219, 305, 626, 657, 664
Phelps, Sylvanus Dryden (1816-1895) W: 279
Pierpoint, Folliott S. (1835-1917) W: 1
Pigott, Jean Sophia (1845-1882) W: 86
Plainsong M: 169, 172
Plumptre, Edward H. (1821-1891) W: 394
Polish Carol M: 194
Pollards, Adelaide A. (1862-1934) W: 400
Pounds, Jessie B. (1861-1921) W: 594
Powell, Robert J. (1932-   ) Arr: 21
Praetorius, Michael (1571-1621)
    Arr: 174

Praxis, Pietatis Melica, (Berlin) (1653) M: 144
Prentiss, Elizabeth P. (1818-1878) W: 476
Prichard, Rowland Hugh (1811-1877) M: 168, 244, 576
Prior, Charles E. (1856-1927) W: 502
Prudentius, Aurelius Clemens (348-413) W: 172
Psalmodia Evangelica M: 239
Psalter, The W: 330
Purvis, Richard (1917-   ) Arr: 6, 169

Quesnel, Steven R. (1950-   ) Arr: 238
Quoist, Michel (1921-   ) R: 383

Rader, Paul (1879-1938) W/M: 585
Rambo, Dottie (1934-   ) W/M: 224
Ramsey, B. Mansell (1849-1923) W/M: 472
Rankin, Jeremiah Eames (1828-1904) W: 523
Raye, Don (1906-   ) W: 693
Redd, Jeff (1935-1984) W: 248, 306, 318, 338, 399, 401, 486, 497, 600, 605
Redhead, Richard (1820-1901) M: 281
Redner, Lewis H. (1831-1908) M: 178
Reed, Andrew (1787-1862) W: 162
Reed, Edith M.G. (1885-1933) W: 194
Rees, John P. (*c.* 1859-   ) W: 107
Reformed Church of America R: 163, 529
Reichardt, C. Luise (*c.* 1780-1826) M: 409
Reid, William W. (1923-   ) R: 93
Reinagle, Alexander R. (1799-1877) M: 229, 685
Rimbault, Edward Francis (1816-1876) M: 647
Ringwald, Roy (1910-   ) Arr: 692
Rinkart, Martin (1586-1649) W: 525
Rippon, John (1751-1836) W: 325, 326, 327
Rist, Johann (1607-1667) W: 207
Roberts, Daniel Crane (1841-1907) W: 687
Roberts, Gladys Westcott (1888-   ) W: 282
Roberts, John (1822-1877) M: 373; Arr: 297
Robinson, George Wade (1838-1877) W: 590
Robinson, Robert (1735-1790) W: 318
Root, George F. (1820-1895) M: 15
Roth, Elton M. (1891-1951) W/M: 633
Rounsefell, Carrie E. (1861-1930) M: 502

ten Boom, Betsie (1885-1944) R: 59
Tennyson, Alfred Lord (1809-1892) R: 441
Teresa, Mother (1910-   ) R: 506
Teschner, Melchoir (1584-1635) M: 249
Theodulph of Orleans (*c*. 760-*c*. 821) W: 249
Thiman, Eric (1900-1975) Arr: 547
Thompson, Van Denman (1890-1969) M: 341
Thompson, Will Lamartine (1847-1909) W/M: 432, 627
Thomson, Mary Ann (1834-1923) W: 658
Threlfall, Jennette (1821-1880) W: 248
Thring, Godfrey (1823-1903) W: 345
Thrupp, Dorothy A. (1779-1847) W: 601
Tolstoy, Leo (1828-1910) R: 403
Tomer, William Gould (1833-1896) M: 523
Toplady, Augustus M. (1740-1778) W: 108
Tourjee, Lizzie S. (1858-1918) M: 115
Tournier, Paul (1898-   ) R: 604
Towner, Daniel Brink (1850-1919) M: 105, 415, 454, 594
Townsend, Frances (1906-   ) W: 315
Traditional W: 234, 361, 591; M: 15, 42, 234, 342, 361, 591; R: 554
Traylor, Champ (1930-   ) R: 549
Troutbeck, Dr. John (1832-1899) W: 207
Trueblood, David Elton (1900-   ) W: 576
Tullar, Grant C. (1869-1950) M: 128
Turner, H.L. (19th century) W: 304

United Church of Christ (1959) R: 141
Unknown . . . see *Anonymous*

Vail, Silas J. (1818-1884) M: 405
Vale, Alliene G. (1918-   ) M: 354
Van de Venter, Judson W. (1855-1939) W: 408
Van Dyke, Henry (1852-1933) W: 377
Vaughan-Williams, Ralph (1872-1958) M: 351, 614; Arr: 208, 537
Virginia Harmony (Carrell and Clayton's) (1831) M: 107

Wade, John F. (1711-1786) W: 193
Wade's John F. *Cantus Diversi* (1711-1786) M: 193
Wagner, Leonard (1900-1973) R: 532
Walch, James (1837-1901) M: 658
Walford, William W. (1772-1850) W: 439
Walter, William Henry (1825-1893) M: 398
Walvoord, John E. (1942-   ) W: 28

Walworth, Clarence A. (1820-1900) W: 385
Ward, Samuel A. (1847-1903) M: 690
Ware, Henry Jr. (1794-1843) W: 540
Waring, Anna Laetitia (1823-1910) W: 489
Warner, Anna Bartlett (1824-1915) W: 226
Warren, George William (1828-1902) M: 687
Watts, Isaac (1674-1748) W: 66, 95, 134, 144, 171, 232, 238, 258, 274, 328, 338, 370, 411, 550
Webb, George J. (1803-1887) M: 616
Webster, George Orlia (1866-1942) W: 450
Weeden, Winfield Scott (1847-1908) M: 408
Weissel, Georg (1590-1635) W: 239
Welsh Melody M: 4, 319, 389, 447, 498
Wesley, Charles (1707-1788) W: 21, 168, 184, 222, 260, 289, 293, 297, 306, 349, 357, 360, 374
Wesley, John (1703-1791) W: 268; R: 640
Wesley, Samuel Sebastian (1810-1876) M: 547, 568
Whitcomb, George Walker (-1910?) W: 310
White's J. T. *"Sacred Harp"* (1844) M: 572
Whitfield, Frederick (1829-1904) W: 634
Whiting, William (1825-1878) W: 679
Whittier, John Greenleaf (1807-1892) W: 422
Whittle, Daniel Webster (1840-1901) W: 65, 580, 631
Wilkinson, Kate B. (1859-1928) W: 483
Willcox, John Henry (1827-1875) M: 335
Williams, C.C. (? -1882) M: 654
Williams, Clara Tear (1858-1937) W: 100
Williams, David McK. (1887-   ) Arr: 323
William's *"New Universal Psalmodist"* (1770?) M: 545

Xavier, Francis (1506-1552) R: 509

Yates, Christina (? - ?) R: 410
Yates, John H. (1837-1900) W: 71
Young, Carlton R. (1926-   ) Arr: 303
Young, G.A. (? - ?) W/M: 597
Young, Gordon (1919-   ) Arr: 376
Young, John F. (1820-1885) W: 195
Young, Ovid (1940-   ) Arr: 67, 335

Zdenek, Marilee (1934-   ) R: 286
Zinzendorf, Nicolaus L. von (1700-1760) W: 268
Zundel, John (1815-1882) M: 21

Collegiate Programs
in Church Music

Ray E. Robinson

Alverno College, 3401 South 39th Street, Milwaukee, Wisconsin 53215
  Sister Mary Hueller, B.M., M.M., D.M.A., Acting Chairman
    Bachelor of Music in Liturgical Music

Augustana College, Rock Island, Illinois 61201
  Ronald F. Jesson, A.B., B.M.E., M.M., Ph.D., Chairman
    Bachelor of Music in Church Music

Baptist College at Charleston, Charleston, South Carolina 29411
  Oliver J. Yost, B.M., M.M., M.S.M., M.R.E., Chairman
    Bachelor of Arts in Music with a Major in Church Music

Barrington College, Barrington, Rhode Island 02806
  Donald E. Brown, B.M., M.S.M., Chairman, Division of Fine Arts
  William I. Han, B.M., M.M., Director, School of Music
    Bachelor of Music in Church Music

Baylor University, Waco, Texas 76703
  Daniel Sternberg, Graduate of Vienna State Academy, Dean,
  School of Music
    Master of Music in Church Music

Belmont College, Nashville, Tennessee 37203
  Jerry L. Warren, B.M., M.S.M., D.M.A., Chairman
    Bachelor of Music in Church Music

Capital University, Conservatory of Music, Columbus, Ohio 43209
  Gerald J. Lloyd, B.M., M.M., Ph.D., Dean
    Bachelor of Music in Church Music

Carson-Newman College, Jefferson City, Tennessee 37760
  Louis O. Ball, Jr., B.A., M.S., M.S.M., D.M.A., Chairman
    Bachelor of Music in Church Music

Catawba College, Salisbury, North Carolina 28144
  Lawrence Bond, Chairman
    Bachelor of Arts in Music (Sacred Music)

Colorado State University, Fort Collins, Colorado 80521
  Robert L. Garretson, A.B., A.M., Ed. D., Chairman
    Master of Music in Church Music

Columbia College, Columbia, South Carolina 29203
  James L. Caldwell, Chairman
    Bachelor of Arts in Church Music

Converse College, Spartanburg, South Carolina 29301
  Henry Janiec, B.M.E., M.M.E., L.H.D., Dean
    Bachelor of Music in Church Music
    Master of Music in Church Music

Cumberland College, Williamsburg, Kentucky 40769
  Harold R. Wortman, B.A., M.A., Ed.D., Head
    Bachelor of Music in Church Music

De Paul University, School of Music, 25 East Jackson Boulevard,
      Chicago, Illinois 60604
  Fredrick S. Miller, B.M.E., M.M., D.M.A., Dean
    Bachelor of Music in Church Music
    Master of Music in Church Music

DePauw University, Greencastle, Indiana 46135
  Donald H. White, B.S., M.M., Ph.D., Director
    Bachelor of Music in Church Music

Drake University, College of Fine Arts, Des Moines, Iowa 50311
  Paul J. Jackson, B.M., M.M., Ph.D., D.F.A., Dean, College of Fine Arts
    Bachelor of Music in Church Music

East Carolina University, Greenville, North Carolina 27834
  Everett Pittman, B.M., M.M., Ph.D., Dean
    Bachelor of Music in Church Music
    Master of Music in Church Music

Eastman School of Music, University of Rochester, Rochester,
      New York 14604
  Robert Freeman, B.A., M.F.A., Ph.D., Director
    Master of Music in Church Music
    Doctor of Musical Arts in Church Music

Furman University, Greenville, South Carolina 29613
  Milburn Price, B.M., M.M., D.M.A., Chairman
    Bachelor of Music in Church Music

Gustavus Adolphus College, Saint Peter, Minnesota 56082
  Paul L. Baumgartner, B.M., M.M., D.M.A., Chairman
    Bachelor of Arts in Church Music

Hardin-Simmons University, Abilene, Texas 79601
    Talmage W. Dean, B.A., B.M., M.M., Ph.D., Dean
        Bachelor of Music in Church Music

Houghton College, Houghton, New York 14744
    Charles H. Finney, A.B., B.M., M.M., Ph.D., F.A.G.O., Chairman
        Bachelor of Music in Church Music

Illinois Wesleyan University, Bloomington, Illinois 61701
    Albert C. Shaw, B.M.E., M.M.E., D.M.E., Director
        Bachelor of Music in Church Music

Indiana University, School of Music, Bloomington, Indiana 47401
    Charles H. Webb, A.B., M.M., Mus. D., Dean
        Master of Music in Church Music

Jacksonville University, Jacksonville, Florida 32211
    Frances Bartlett Kinne, B.M.E., M.M.E., Ph.D., Dean
        Bachelor of Music in Church Music

Jordan College of Music of Butler University, 46th and Clarendon,
    Indianapolis, Indiana 46208
    Louis F. Chenette, B.A., M.M., Ph.D., Dean
        Master of Sacred Music (offered jointly with the Christian Theologi-
        cal Seminary)

Kent State University, Kent, Ohio 44242
    James L. Waters, B.M., M.M., Ph.D., Acting Director, School of Music
        Bachelor of Music in Sacred Music
        Master of Arts in Sacred Music

Louisiana State University, Baton Rouge, Louisiana 70803
    Everett Timm, B.M., M.M., Ph. D., D.M., Dean
        Bachelor of Music in Sacred Music

Louisiana Tech University, Ruston, Louisiana 71270
    Raymond G. Young, B.M., M.M., Head
        Bachelor of Fine Arts in Sacred Music

Mars Hill College, Mars Hill, North Carolina 28754
    E. Wayne Pressley, B.A., M.A., D.M.A., Acting Chairman
        Bachelor of Music in Church Music

Marywood College, Scranton, Pennsylvania 18509
    Jane E. McGowty, B.A., M.A., Chairperson
        Bachelor of Music in Church Music

Memphis State University, Memphis, Tennessee 38111
    Robert A. Snyder, B.S., M.S., D.M., Chairman
        Bachelor of Music in Church Music

Milliken University, School of Music, Decatur, Illinois 62526
   Clayton W. Henderson, B.F.A., M.F.A., Ph.D., Dean
      Bachelor of Music in Church Music

Mississippi College, Clinton, Mississippi 39056
   Jack Lyall, B.F.A., M.M., Ed.D., Head
      Bachelor of Music in Church Music

Mount St. Mary's College, Los Angeles, California 90049
   Sister Teresita, D.M.A., Chairman
      Bachelor of Music in Church Music

New England Conservatory of Music, 290 Huntington Avenue, Boston,
    Massachusetts 02115
   Gunther Schuller, President
      Master of Music in Church Music

New Orleans Baptist Theological Seminary, 3939 Gentilly Boulevard,
    New Orleans, Louisiana 70126
   Clinton C. Nichols, B.M.E., M.S.M., D.M., Chairman
      Master of Church Music
      Doctor of Education in Church Music Education

Northwestern University, School of Music, Evanston, Illinois 60201
   Thomas W. Miller, B.S., M.A., Mus.A.D., Dean
      Bachelor of Music in Church Music
      Master of Music in Church Music
      Doctor of Music in Church Music

Nyack College, Nyack, New York 10960
   Paul F. Liljestrand, B.M., M.M., M.S.M., Chairman
      Bachelor of Sacred Music

Ohio State University, Columbus, Ohio 43210
   Andrew J. Broekema, B.M., M.M., Ph.D., Dean, College of the Arts
      Bachelor of Music in Church Music
      Master of Music in Church Music

Oklahoma Baptist University, Shawnee, Oklahoma 74801
   James D. Woodward, B.M., M.S.M., Dean, College of Fine Arts
      Bachelor of Music in Church Music

Oklahoma City University, School of Music, Oklahoma City, Oklahoma
    73106
   Fred C. Mayer, B.M., M.A., D.Mus., Dean
      Bachelor of Music in Church Music

Ouachita Baptist University, Arkadelphia, Arkansas 71923
   William E. Trantham, B.S., B.S.E., M.M., Ph.D., Dean
      Bachelor of Music in Church Music

Pfeiffer College, Misenheimer, North Carolina 28109
Stanley R. Scheer, B.M., M.M., Chairman
Bachelor of Arts with Major in Music (Church Music)

Philadelphia College of the Bible, Philadelphia, Pennsylvania 19103
Alfred E. Lunde, B.A. in Ed., Th.M., M. Mus., Chairman
Bachelor of Music in Church Music

St. Andrews Presbyterian College, Laurinburg, North Carolina 28352
James V. Cobb, Jr., A.B., B.M., M.A., D.M.A., Director
Bachelor of Music in Church Music

St. Olaf College, Northfield, Minnesota 55057
Adolph White, B.S., M.M., Ph.D., Chairman
Bachelor of Music in Church Music

Samford University, Birmingham, Alabama 35209
Claude H. Rhea, A.B., B.M.E., M.M.E., Ed.D., Dean
Bachelor of Music in Church Music

Seattle Pacific University, Seattle, Washington 98119
Wayne H. Balch, A.B., M.M., Director
Bachelor of Arts in Church Music

Shenandoah College and Conservatory of Music, Winchester, Virginia
22601
Verne E. Collins, B.S., M.M., Ed.D., Dean
Bachelor of Music in Church Music

Shorter College, Rome, Georgia 30161
John Ramsaur, B.M., M.M., Head
Bachelor of Music in Church Music

Southern Baptist Theological Seminary, Louisville, Kentucky 40206
Forrest H. Heeren, B.S., M.S., M.A., Ed.D., Dean
Master of Music in Church Music
Doctor of Musical Arts in Church Music

Southern Methodist University, Dallas, Texas 75275
J. William Hipp, B.M., M.M., Chairman
Master of Sacred Music (with Perkins School of Theology)

Southwestern at Memphis, 2000 North Parkway, Memphis, Tennessee
38112
Charles Mosby, B.M., M.M., Chairman
Bachelor of Music in Sacred Music

Southwestern Baptist Theological Seminary, Fort Worth, Texas 76122
  James C. McKinney, B.M., M.M., D.M.A., Dean
    Master of Church Music
    Master of Music in Church Music
    Doctor of Musical Arts in Church Music

Southwestern University, Georgetown, Texas 78626
  Theodore D. Lucas, Dean, School of Fine Arts
    Bachelor of Music in Church Music

State University College, Potsdam, New York 13676
  Robert W. Thayer, B.M., M.M.E., Ph.D., Acting Dean
    Bachelor of Music in Church Music

Stetson University, Deland, Florida 32720
  Paul T. Langston, B.A., M.S.M., S.M.D., Dean
    Bachelor of Music in Church Music

Susquehanna University, Selinsgrove, Pennsylvania 17870
  James B. Steffy, B.S., Mus.Ed., M.Mus.Ed., Chairman, Dept. of Music
    Bachelor of Music in Church Music

Texas Christian University, Fort Worth, Texas 76129
  Michael Winesanker, Mus.Bac., L.Mus.T.C.L., M.A., Ph.D., Chair-
    man, Department of Music
    Bachelor of Music in Church Music

Trevecca Nazarene College, 333 Murfreesboro Road, Nashville, Tennes-
    see 32710
  Barbara McClain, Chairman
    Bachelor of Science in Church Music

Union University, Jackson, Tennessee 38301
  Kenneth R. Hartley, B.S.M.E., M.S.M., Ed.D., Head, Dept. of Music
    Bachelor of Music in Sacred Music

University of Colorado, College of Music, Boulder, Colorado 80302
  Warner L. Imig, A.B., M.Mus.Ed., Dean
    Bachelor of Music in Church Music

University of Louisville, School of Music, Louisville, Kentucky 40222
  Jerry W. Ball, B.M.E., M.M., Dean
    Bachelor of Music in Organ—Church Music

University of Puget Sound, Tacoma, Washington 98416
  Bruce Rodgers, B.M., M.M., Ph.D., Director
    Bachelor of Music in Church Music
    Master of Music in Church Music

University of Redlands, Redlands, California 92373
Wayne R. Bohrnstedt, B.M., M.M., Ph.D., F.I.A.L., Director
Bachelor of Music in Church Music

University of Southern California, University Park, Los Angeles, California 90007
Grant Beglarian, B.M., M.M., D.M.A., Dean, School of Performing Arts
Bachelor of Music in Church Music
Master of Music in Church Music
Doctor of Musical Arts in Church Music

University of Southern Mississippi, Hattiesburg, Mississippi 39401
Vivian P. Wood, B.M., M.M., Ph.D., Acting Dean, School of Fine Arts
Bachelor of Music in Church Music

University of Tennessee at Chattanooga, 725 Oak Street, Chattanooga, Tennessee 37403
Peter E. Gerschefski, A.B., A.M., Ph.D., Chairman
Bachelor of Music in Church Music

University of Texas, Austin, Texas 78712
Peter Garvie, B.A., M.A., Dean
Bachelor of Music in Church Music

Valparaiso University, Valparaiso, Indiana 46383
Frederick Telschow, B.A., M.M., D.M.A., Chairman
Bachelor of Music in Church Music

Virginia Commonwealth University, 901 West Franklin Street, Richmond, Virginia 23284
Ronald B. Thomas, B.M., M.M., Chairman
Bachelor of Music in Church Music

Wayne State University, Detroit, Michigan 48202
Robert F. Lawson, M.A., Chairman
Bachelor of Music in Church Music

Wesleyan College, Macon, Georgia 31201
Sylvia L. Ross, B.S., S.M.M., D.M.A., Chairman
Bachelor of Music in Church Music

West Virginia Wesleyan College, Buckhannon, West Virginia 26201
Bobby H. Loftis, B.M., M.M., Ph.D., Chairman
Bachelor of Arts in Church Music

Westminster Choir College, Princeton, New Jersey 08540
Ray E. Robinson, B.A., M.M., D.M.E., President
Bachelor of Music in Church Music

Westminster College, New Wilmington, Pennsylvania
  Clarence J. Martin, B.M., M.M., D.M.A., Chairman
    Bachelor of Music in Church Music

William Carey College, Hattiesburg, Mississippi 39401
  Donald Winters, B.M., M.M., D.Mus., Dean
    Bachelor of Music in Church Music
    Master of Music in Church Music

Wittenberg University, Springfield, Ohio 45501
  L. David Miller, A.B., M.Div., M.S.M., Mus.D., Dean
    Bachelor of Music in Church Music
    Master of Sacred Music

Yankton College, Yankton, South Dakota 57078
  George B. Whaley, B.A., M.M., Ed.D., Director
    Bachelor of Music in Church Music

Church Music References
and Workshops

Ray E. Robinson

ALABAMA
UNIVERSITY
Write: Director, Continuing Education in Arts and Sciences, P.O. Box 2967, University, AL 35286

CALIFORNIA
FULLERTON
Choral Conductor's Guild of California, State Convention at California State University.
Write: P.O. Box 15294, Long Beach, CA 90815
FULLERTON
Annual Western States Music Clinic at California State University. Twenty-nine distinguished clinicians.
Write: Keynote Music Service, 833 South Olive Street, Los Angeles, CA 90014. Phone (213) 627-4837.
LOS ANGELES
Lutheran Institute for Worship and Music at UCLA and University Lutheran Chapel. Sponsored jointly by the Lutheran Church in America (Division for Parish Services), The Lutheran Church-Missouri Synod (Commission of Worship), and the American Lutheran Church (Division for Life and Mission in the Congregation). Sessions for organists, choir directors, parish pastors, lay parish worship leaders and synod and district leaders. Seasonal theme: Holy Week and Lent, Easter Season through the Day of Pentecost.
Write: Lutheran Institutes for Worship and Music, 422 South Fifth Street Minneapolis, MN 55415. Phone (612) 338-3821.
LOS ANGELES
Church Music Clinic. Location to be selected. Sessions morning only.
Choral reading, adult and children's choir.
Write: Augsburg Publishing House, 3224 Beverly Boulevard, Los Angeles, CA 90057. Phone (213) 386-3722.

COLORADO
DENVER
Lutheran Institute for Worship and Music at Colorado Women's College.
See under Los Angeles, California for details.
DENVER
Paul Christiansen Choral Workshop at University of Denver.
Write: Concordia College, Moorhead, MN 56560.

ILLINOIS
DECATUR
Paul Christiansen Choral Workshop at Millikin University.
Write: Concordia College, Moorhead, MN 56560.

INDIANA
RENSSELAER
Write: Director, Rensselaer Program of Church Music and Liturgy, Saint Joseph's College, Rensselaer, IN 47978.

MAINE
WATERVILLE
Annual Church Music Institute, at Colby College
Sessions: chorus, conducting, organ and piano.
Write: Director, Special Programs, Colby College, Waterville, ME 04901.

MARYLAND
BALTIMORE
Annual North American Institute on Worship and Music at Saint Mary's Seminary and University, Roland Park. Theme: Ministries in Parish Worship.
Write: Music Institute, 5400 Roland Avenue, Baltimore, MD 21210.

MICHIGAN
ANN ARBOR
Lutheran Institute for Worship and Music at Concordia College.
See under Los Angeles, California for details.
EAST LANSING
Church Music Workshop at Michigan State University.
Write: 24 Kellogg Center for Continuing Education, Michigan State University, East Lansing, MI 48824.

MINNESOTA
BEMIDJI
Paul Christiansen Choral Workshop at Bemidji State University.
Write: Concordia College, Moorhead, MN 56560.
NORTHFIELD
Choristers Guild Workshop at St. Olaf College.
Write: Choristers Guild, P.O. Box 38188, Dallas, TX 75238.

NEW HAMPSHIRE
WEST SWANZEY
Church Music Workshop at Pilgrim Pines.
Write: Pilgrim Pines, West Swanzey, NH 03469.

NEW JERSEY
PRINCETON
Vocal Festivals and Workshops in Church Music at Westminster
Choir College, Princeton, New Jersey. Two graduate credits are
available for each workshop. For Application and Catalog,
Write: Director of Summer Session, Westminster Choir College,
Princeton, NJ 08540.
PRINCETON
World Library presents summer workshop sponsored by the Liturgy
Office of the Diocese of Trenton, at Princeton University.
Write: Liturgy Office, P.O. Box 3246, Trenton, NJ 08619.

NEW YORK
ALFRED
Annual Alfred Church Music Institute of Alfred University. Ses-
sions: junior and senior choirs, organ, handbells, and carillon,
concerts, receptions and banquet.
Write: Box 762, Alfred, NY 14802. Phone (607) 587-2325.
CHAUTAUQUA
Paul Christiansen Choral Workshop at Chautauqua Institute.
Write: Concordia College, Moorhead, MN 56560.

NORTH CAROLINA
ARDEN
School of Church Music and Worship at Lutheridge Camp and
Conference Center.
Write: Lutheridge, P.O. Box 685, Arden, NC 28704.

OHIO
SPRINGFIELD
Coordinated by the Presbyterian Association of Musicians, at Wittenburg University.
Write: 21 N. Chillicothe Street, South Charleston, OH 45368.
WORTHINGTON
Church Music Clinic at Worthington United Methodist Church. Sponsored by Augsburg Publishing House. Sessions: choral, organ and handbell.
Write: Augsburg Publishing House, 57 East Main Street, Columbus, OH 43215. Phone (614) 221-7411.

PENNSYLVANIA
ALLENTOWN
Lutheran Institute for Worship and Music at Muhlenberg College. See under Los Angeles, California for details.
BRYN MAWR
Krisheim VI sponsored by the Philadelphia Chapter, American Guild of Organists, at Bryn Mawr Presbyterian Church.
Write: 224 Fisher Road, Jenkintown, PA 19046. (215) 884-2574.
EAST STROUDSBURG
The Fred Waring Music Workshop Youth Choral sessions at East Stroudsburg State College. For young musicians 15 through college age. Up to three college credits available.
Write: Managing Director, Fred Waring Music Workshop, Delaware Water Gap, PA 18327.
EAST STROUDSBURG
The Fred Waring Music Workshop Adult Choral Workshops at East Stroudsburg State College. Up to 6 graduate or undergraduate credits available.
Write: Managing Director, Fred Waring Music Workshop, Delaware Water Gap, PA 18327.
LAFAYETTE HILL
Church Music Institute for the Southeastern Pennsylvania Synod at St. Peter's Lutheran Church.
Write: St. Peter's Lutheran Church, 3025 Church Road, Lafayette Hill, PA 19444.

SOUTH CAROLINA
NEWBERRY
Lutheran Institute for Worship and Music at Newberry College. See under Los Angeles, California for details.

TEXAS
HOUSTON
Paul Christiansen Choral Workshop at Houston Baptist University.
Write: Concordia College, Moorhead, MN 56560
SAN ANTONIO
Choristers Guild Workshop at Trinity University.
Write: Choristers Guild, P.O. Box 38188, Dallas, TX 75238.
SEGUIN
Lutheran Institute for Worship and Music at Texas Lutheran College.
See under Los Angeles, California for details.

WASHINGTON
SEATTLE
The Annual North American Institute on Worship and Music at Saint Thomas Seminary, Kenmore.
Write: Institute, 5400 Roland Avenue, Baltimore, MD 21210.
SEATTLE
Church Music Clinic at Plymouth Congregational Church.
Sponsored by Augsburg Publishing House. Sessions: choral and organ.
Write: Augsburg Publishing House, 2001 Third Avenue, Seattle, WA 98121. Phone (206) 624-0244.
TACOMA
Lutheran Institute for Worship and Music at Pacific Lutheran University. See under Los Angeles, California for details.

WISCONSIN
DARLINGTON
Music workshop presented by the University of Wisconsin at Immanuel United Church of Christ. Sessions: choral and organ, hymn and service playing, youth choirs, Sunday school music, conducting and organ techniques, handbell choirs and laboratory sessions.
Write: UW-Extension Music, 610 Langdon Street, Madison, WI 53706.
GREEN LAKE
The Annual Conference of Church Musicians, sponsored by the Fellowship of American Baptist Musicians at the American Baptist Assembly.
Write: President, Fellowship of American Baptist Musicians, American Baptist Churches of USA, Valley Forge, PA 19481.

MADISON
  Annual Church Music Conference presented by the University of Wisconsin Extension Music at Bethel Lutheran Church.
  Write: UW-Extension Music, 610 Langdon Street, Madison, WI 53706.
MANITOWOC
  Music workshop presented by the University of Wisconsin at Holy Innocents Catholic Church. Sessions: choral and organ, hymn and service playing, youth choirs, Sunday school music, conducting and organ techniques, handbell choirs and laboratory sessions.
  Write: UW-Extension Music, 610 Langdon Street, Madison, WI 53706.
RICE LAKE
  Music workshop presented by the University of Wisconsin at Bethany Lutheran Church. Sessions: choral and organ, hymn and service playing, youth choirs, Sunday school music, conducting and organ techniques, handbell choirs and laboratory sessions.
  Write: UW-Extension Music, 610 Langdon Street, Madison, WI 53706.
WEST ALLIS
  Music workshop presented by the University of Wisconsin at Apostle United Presbyterian Church. Sessions: choral and organ, hymn and service playing, youth choirs, Sunday school music, conducting and organ techniques, handbell choirs and laboratory sessions.
  Write: UW-Extension Music, 610 Langdon Street, Madison, WI 53706.

CANADA
  WATERLOO, ONTARIO
  Lutheran Institute for Worship and Music at Wilfred Laurier University.
  See under Los Angeles, California for details.
NOTE:
Music publishers often have workshops in which they demonstrate new and innovative tools for aiding worship, education and evangelism. See listing of Church Music Publishers, page 254.

Suggested Books and Periodicals Concerning Church Music, Hymnology and Related Areas

Fred Bock and Bryan Jeffrey Leech

BOOKS

ASCAP Biographical Dictionary of Composers, Authors, and Publishers, Ed. The Lynn Farnol Group, Inc., NY: American Society of Composers, Authors, and Publishers, 1966.

Bailey, Albert Edward. *The Gospel in Hymns*, NY: Charles Scribner's Sons, 1950.

Baker's Biographical Dictionary of Musicians, Ed. Nicolas Slonimsky, NY: G. Schirmer, 1958, Supplement 1965.

Barrows, Cliff, and Hustad, Donald P. *Crusader Hymns and Hymn Stories*, Carol Stream, IL: Hope Publishing Company, 1967.

The Book of Common Prayer, NY: The Church Pension Fund, 1945.

Bucke, Emory Stevens, Ed. *Companion to the Hymnal — a handbook to the 1964 Methodist Hymnal*, Nashville: Abingdon Press, 1970.

Chase, Gilbert. *America's Music: From Pilgrims to the Present*, 2nd edition, revised. NY: McGraw-Hill Book Co., 1966.

Christensen, James I. *Don't Waste Your Time in Worship*, Old Tappan, NJ: Fleming H. Revell Co., 1978.

Davidson, James Robert. *A Dictionary of Protestant Church Music*, Metuchen, NJ: Scarecrow Press, 1975.

Douglas, Winfred. *Church Music in History and Practice*, NY: Charles Scribner's Sons, 1937, Revised 1962.

Erickson, J. Irving. *Twice-Born Hymns*, Chicago: Covenant Press, 1977.

Ertherington, Charles L. *Protestant Worship Music*, NY: Holt, Rinehart and Winston, 1962.

Haeussler, Armin. *The Story of Our Hymns*, St. Louis: Eden Publishing House, 1952.

Hustad, Donald P. *Dictionary-Handbook to "Hymns of the Living Church"*, Carol Stream, IL: Hope Publishing Company, 1978.

Hymns Ancient and Modern (Historical Edition), London: William Clowes & Sons, Ltd., 1909.

Jacobs, Arthur. *Choral Music*, Baltimore: Penguin Books, 1963.

Julian, John. *A Dictionary of Hymnology*, 2nd edition revised, 1907. Dover Books, 1957.

McCutchan, Robert Guy. *Hymn Tune Names*, Nashville: Abingdon Press, 1964.

Martin-Hugh, Ed. *The Baptist Hymn Book Companion*, London: Psalms and Hymns Trust, 1962

Mees, Arthur. *Choirs and Choral Music*, NY: Charles Scribner's Sons, 1924.

Metcalf, Frank J. *American Writers and Compilers Of Sacred Music*, NY: Abingdon Press, 1925.

Nardone, Thomas R., Nye, James H., Resnick, Mark. *Choral Music in Print, Vol. I: Sacred Choral Music*, Philadelphia: Musicdata, Inc., 1974.

————. *Choral Music in Print*, 1976 Supplement, Philadelphia: Musicdata, Inc., 1976.

Ortlund, Anne. *Up With Worship*, Glendale, CA: Gospel Light Publications, 1975.

Palack, W.G. *The Handbook to the Lutheran Hymal*, St. Louis: Concordia Publishing House, 1942.

Parker, Alice. *Creative Hymn Singing*, Chapel Hill, NC: Hinshaw Music, Inc., 1976.

Reynolds, William Jensen. *Hymns of Our Faith*, Nashville: Broadman Press, 1964.

————. *Companion to the Baptist Hymnal*, Nashville: Broadman Press, 1977.

Romander, Albert C., Porter, Ethel K. *Guide to the Pilgrim Hymal*, Philadelphia: United Church Press, 1966.

Routley, Erik. *Twentieth Century Church Music*, NY: Oxford University Press, 1964.

————. Ed. *Westminster Praise*, Chapel Hill, NC: Hinshaw Music, Inc., 1977.

————. *Companion to "Westminster Praise"*, Chapel Hill, NC: Hinshaw Music, Inc., 1977.

Stevenson, Robert. *Protestant Church Music In America*, NY: The Free Press (Macmillan), 1970.

Ward, Ruth. *Worship is for Kids, Too!* Kalamazoo, MI: Master's Press, Inc., 1976.

Wiendant, Elwyn A., *Choral Music of the Church*, NY: The Free Press (Macmillan), 1965.

Wiendant, Elwyn A., and Young, Robert H. *The Anthem in England and America*, NY: The Free Press (Macmillan), 1970.

Work, John W. *American Negro Songs & Spirituals*, NY: Bonanza Books, 1940.
Young, Carlton R., Ed. and others. *Ecumenical Praise*, Carol Stream, IL: Hope Publishing Company, 1977.

PERIODICALS

"The American Organist", 630 Fifth Avenue, New York, NY 10020
"The Choral Journal", Journal of the American Choral Director's Association, 1902 Association Dr., Reston, VA 22091
"Church Music", Concordia Publishing House, 3558 S. Jefferson, St. Louis, MO 63118
"Creator", Creative Church Music Society, P.O. Box 7714, Wichita, KS 67277
"Diapason", 434 S. Wabash Ave., Chicago, IL 60605
"The Hymn", Journal of the Hymn Society of America, National Headquarters, Wittenberg University, Springfield, OH 45501
Hymn Society of Great Britain & Ireland, Ed. Dr. Bernard S. Massey, 23 Ridgeway Rd., Redhill, Surrey, England RH1 6PQ
"Journal" of Choral Conductor's Guild, 4519 Los Feliz #307, Los Angeles, CA 90027
"Journal of Church Music", Fortress Press, 2900 Queen Lane, Philadelphia, PA 19129
"Music Ministry", United Methodist Publishing House, 201 8th Ave., S., Nashville, TN 37202
"Reformed Liturgy and Music", United Presbyterian Church, Witherspoon Building, Philadelphia, PA 19129
"Sacred Music", 3800 Crystal Lake Blvd., Minneapolis, MN 55422
"Worship & Arts", 11392 Wallingsford Rd., Los Alamitos, CA 90720

Names and Addresses of Church Music Publishers and Distributors

AMP
  866 Third Avenue
  New York, NY 10022
  Distributed by G. Schirmer, Inc.

AMSCO
  33 West 60th Street
  New York, NY 10023

ASCAP
  1 Lincoln Plaza
  New York, NY 10023

ABINGDON PRESS
  201 Eighth Avenue, S.
  Nashville, TN 37203

AGAPÉ
  Carol Stream, IL 60187
  Distributed by Hope Publishing
  Company

ALEXANDRIA HOUSE
  Box 300
  Alexandria, IN 46001

ALSBACH & DOYER
  De Eerste Muziekcentrale N.V.
  P.O. Box 338 Bussem, Netherlands
  Distributed by C. F. Peters Corp.

AMERICAN COMPOSER'S
    ALLIANCE
  585 Fifth Avenue
  New York, NY 10023

ARS NOVA
  Oostsingle #9
  Postrekening 81245 Goes, Holland
  Distributed by Theodore Presser Co.

ASSOCIATED MUSIC PUBLISHERS
  see AMP

AUGENER
  82 Hi Road
  East Finchley, London, N2 9PH,
    England
  Distributed by Galaxy Music Corp.

AUGSBURG PUBLISHING HOUSE
  426 S. 5th Street
  Minneapolis, MN 55415

AVANT
  2859 Holt Avenue
  Los Angeles, CA 90034
  Distributed by Western International
    Music

BMI
  40 W. 57th Street
  New York, NY 10019

M. BAHN
  Heinrichshofen, Germany

BÄRENREITER
  Heinrich Schutz Allee
  Postfach 10-03-29 D. E-3500 Kassel,
    Germany
  Distributed by Magnamusic-Baton

BEACON HILL MUSIC
  Box 527
  Kansas City, MO 64141
  Distributed by Lillenas Publishing
    Co.

BECKENHORST PRESS
  Box 14275
  Columbus, OH 43214

BELWIN-MILLS MUSIC CORP.
  Melville, NY 11746

BENSON PUBLISHING COMPANY
325 Great Circle Drive
Nashville, TN 37205

FRED BOCK MUSIC COMPANY
Box 333
Tarzana, CA 91356
Distributed by Alexandria House

BOOSEY & HAWKES
Oceanside, NY 11572

BOSTON MUSIC COMPANY
122 Boylston Street
Boston, MA 02116

BOTE & BOCK
Hardenberg Strasse
9a 1 Berlin 12, Germany
Distributed by G. Schirmer

BOURNE, INC.
1212 Avenue of Americas
New York, NY 10022
Distributed by G. Schirmer

BREITKOPF & HÄRTEL
Walkühl Strasse
52 D. 6200 Wiesbaden, W. Germany
Distributed by G. Schirmer

BROADMAN PRESS
127 Ninth Avenue, N.
Nashville, TN 37203

BRODT MUSIC COMPANY
1408 Independence Blvd.
Charlotte, NC 28201

CARL FISCHER, INC.
62 Cooper Square
New York, NY 10003

CENTURY MUSIC
    PUBLISHING CO.
263 Veterans Boulevard
Carlsbad, NJ 07072

CHANCEL MUSIC, INC.
1634 Spruce Street
Philadelphia, PA 19003
Distributed by Walfred Publishing
Co.

CHORISTER'S GUILD
Box 38188
Dallas, TX 75238

CONCORDIA PUBLISHING HOUSE
3558 Jefferson Avenue
St. Louis, MO 62118

J. B. CRAMER & CO. LTD.
99 St. Martin's Lane
London, WC2 England
Distributed by Brodt Music Co.

CRESCENDO MUSIC PUBLISHERS
2580 Gus Thomasson Road
Dallas, TX 75228

CURWEN
140 Strand
London, England
Distributed by G. Schirmer

OLIVER DITSON
Presser Place
Bryn Mawr, PA 19010
Distributed by Theodore Presser
Company

ELKAN-VOGEL
Presser Place
Bryn Mawr, PA 19010
Distributed by Theodore Presser Company

ELKINS
145 Palisades Street
Dobbs Ferry, NY 10522
Distributed by Novello

ETHEL SMITH MUSIC CORP.
1842 West Avenue
Miami Beach, FL 33139
Distributed by Hansen Publications,
Inc.

EUROPEAN-AMERICAN MUSIC
    DISTRIBUTORS CORP.
195 Allwood Rd.
Clifton, NJ 07012

F.E.L. PUBLICATIONS, LTD.
1925 S. Pontius Avenue
Los Angeles, CA 90025

F. W. GADOW & SON
Hildbur Ghaussen, Germany

J. FISCHER
Melville, NY 11746
Distributed by Belwin-Mills Music
Corp.

H. T. FITZSIMONS
615 N. La Salle Street
Chicago, IL 60610

HAROLD FLAMMER, INC.
Delaware Water Gap, PA 18327
Distributed by Shawnee Press, Inc.

MARK FOSTER MUSIC COMPANY
Box 4012
Champaign, IL 61820

FOX MUSIC PUBLICATIONS
Box 333
Tarzana, CA 91356
Distributed by Alexandria House

SAM FOX PUBLISHING COMPANY
Box 850
Valley Forge, PA 19482

GAITHER MUSIC COMPANY
Box 300
Alexandria, IN 46001
Distributed by Alexandria House

GALAXY MUSIC CORP.
2121 Broadway
New York, NY 10023

GENTRY PUBLICATIONS
Box 333
Tarzana, CA 91356
Distributed by Hinshaw Music, Inc.

GLORYSOUND
Delaware Water Gap, PA 18327
Distributed by Shawnee Press, Inc.

GOSPEL PUBLISHING HOUSE
1445 Boonville Avenue
Springfield, MO 65802

H. W. GRAY
Melville, NY 11746
Distributed by
Belwin-Mills Music Corp.

HAMBLEN MUSIC COMPANY
19th Ave. No. & Hayes St.
Nashville, TN 37202
Distributed by Alexandria House

HANSEN PUBLICATIONS, INC.
1842 West Avenue
Miami Beach, FL 33139

HEULENHAGER & GRIEHL
Hamburg, Germany

HINRICHSEN EDITION LIMITED
10-12 Baches Street
London, NI 6DN, England
Distributed by C. F. Peters Corp.

HINSHAW MUSIC, INC.
Box 470
Chapel Hill, NC 27514

HOPE PUBLISHING CO.
Carol Stream, IL 60187

JACK SPRATT MUSIC
170 N.E. 33 Street
Ft. Lauderdale, FL 33307
Distributed by Plymouth Music
Corp.

KAISER
Munich, Germany

NEIL A KJOS MUSIC COMPANY
4382 Jutland Drive
San Diego, CA 92117

KRUMPHOLZ & CO.
Bern, Switzerland

LAWSON-GOULD MUSIC
PUBLISHERS
866 Third Avenue
New York, NY 10022
Distributed by G. Schirmer

LEEDS MUSIC
445 Park Avenue
New York, NY 10022
Distributed by MCA Music

ALFRED LENGNICK & CO., INC.
Purley Oaks *STUS*
421-A Brighton Rd.
S. Croydon
London, England

LEUKART
Wibelungen Straase
48 8000 Munich, 19 W. Germany
Distributed by G. Schirmer

LEXICON MUSIC, INC.
Box 296
Woodland Hills, CA 91364
Distributed by Word, Inc.

LILLENAS PUBLISHING COMPANY
Box 527
Kansas City, MO 64141

LITURGICAL MUSIC PRESS
Presser Place
Bryn Mawr, PA 19010
Distributed by Theodore Presser

LORENZ INDUSTRIES
501 E. Third Street
Dayton, OH 45401

MCA MUSIC
445 Park Avenue
New York, NY 10022

McAFEE MUSIC
300 East 59th Street
New York, NY 10022
Distributed by Lorenz Industries

McLAUGHLIN & REILLY
1834 Ridge Avenue
Evanston, IL 60204
Distributed by Summy Publishing
Co.

MAGNAMUSIC-BATON, INC.
10370 Page Industrial Boulevard
St. Louis, MO 63132

MANNA MUSIC, INC.
2111 Kenmere Avenue
Burbank, CA 91504

E. B. MARKS MUSIC CORP.
1790 Broadway
New York, NY 10019
Distributed by Belwin-Mills Music
Corp.

MERCURY MUSIC CORP.
Presser Place
Bryn Mawr, PA 19010
Distributed by Theodore Presser

WILLY MEULLER COMPANY
Sueddeutscher Musikverlag
Maerzgase 5
Heidelberg, Germany
Distributed by C. F. Peters Corp.

NOVELLO
145 Palisades Street
Dobbs Ferry, NY 10522

OXFORD UNIVERSITY PRESS
200 Madison Avenue
New York, NY 10019

PARAGON ASSOCIATES, INC.
19th Ave. No. & Hayes St.
Nashville, TN 37202
Distributed by Alexandia House

PAXTON
145 Palisades Street
Dobbs Ferry, NY 10522
Distributed by Novello

C. F. PETERS CORP.
373 Park Avenue, S.
New York, NY 10016

PLYMOUTH MUSIC CORP.
170 N.E. 33 Street
Ft. Lauderdale, FL 33307

THEODORE PRESSER COMPANY
Presser Place
Bryn Mawr, PA 19010

PRO-ART PUBLICATIONS, INC.
Melville, NY 11746
Distributed by Belwin-Mills Music Corp.

RICHARDS & CO.
London, England

R. D. ROW
62 Cooper Square
New York, NY 10003
Distributed by Carl Fischer, Inc.

SESAC
10 Columbus Circle
New York, NY 10019

SACRED MANUSCRIPTS
325 Great Circle Drive
Nashville, TN 37205
Distributed by Benson Publishing Co.

SACRED MUSIC PRESS
501 E. Third Street
Dayton, OH 45401

SACRED SONGS
Box 1790
Waco, TX 76703
Distributed by Word, Inc.

E. C. SCHIRMER MUSIC COMPANY
600 Washington Street
Boston, MA 02111

G. SCHIRMER
866 Third Avenue
New York, NY 10022

SCHMIDT
1834 Ridge Avenue
Evanston, IL 60204
Distributed by Summy Publishing
Co.

SCHMITT, HALL & McCREARY
Melville, NY 11746
Distributed by Belwin-Mills
Music Corp.

SCHOTT
195 Allwood Road
Clifton, NJ 07012
Distributed by European-American

SCHUBERTH
263 Veterans Boulevard
Carlsbad, NJ 07072
Distributed by Century Music
Publishing Co.

SHATTINGER INTERNATIONAL
1842 West Avenue
Miami Beach, FL 33139

SHAWNEE PRESS, INC.
Delaware Water Gap, PA 18327

SINGSPIRATION, INC.
4145 Kalamazoo Avenue, S.E.
Grand Rapids, MI 49508
Distributed by Zondervan
Publishing House

SOMERSET PUBLICATIONS
Carol Stream, IL 60187
Distributed by Hope Publishing Co.

SOUTHERN MUSIC COMPANY
Box 329
San Antonio, TX 78292

STAINER & BELL
82 Hi Road,
East Fincheley, London, N2 9PN,
England
Distributed by Galaxy Music Corp.

STAMPS-BAXTER MUSIC
201 S. Tyler
Dallas, TX 75208
Distributed by Zondervan
Publishing House

STEINGRÄBER
Offenbach/M
62 Wiesbaden, Postfach 471
West Germany

SUMMY PUBLISHING COMPANY
1834 Ridge Avenue
Evanston, IL 60204

GORDON V. THOMPSON, LTD.
29 Alcorn Avenue
Toronto, Ontario, Canada M4V 1E2

TRIUNE MUSIC, INC.
824 Nineteenth Avenue, S.
Nashville, TN 37203

WALFRED PUBLISHING COMPANY
1634 Spruce Street
Philadelphia, PA 19003

WALTON MUSIC CORP.
501 E. Third Street
Dayton, OH 45401
Distributed by Lorenz Industries

WARNER BROS. PUBLICATIONS
265 Secaucus Road
Secaucus, NJ 07094

WATERLOO
3 Regina St. North
Waterloo, Ontario N. 2J 2Z7
Distributed by G. Schirmer

WEEKES & CO.
London, England

WESTERN INTERNATIONAL MUSIC
2859 Holt Avenue
Los Angeles, CA 90034

WITMARK
see Warner Bros. Publications

WORD, INC.
Box 1790
Waco, TX 76703

WORLD LIBRARY PUBLICATIONS,
INC.
2145 Central Parkway
Cincinnati, OH 45214

ZONDERVAN PUBLISHING HOUSE
1415 Lake Drive, S.E.
Grand Rapids, MI 49506